# I am so *happy*

Sky Hawk

Published by Uiri Press 2016
First edition, first printing

Design and writing © 2016 Sky Hawk

Photo credit: <a href="http://www.flickr.com/photos /82955120@N05/15933205475">Winter Daisy - HDR</a> via <a href="http://photopin.com">photopin</a> <a href="https://creativecommons.org/licenses/by/2.0 /">(license)</a>

All rights reserved. No part of this book may be reproduced or transmitted in any form or by any means, including but not limited to information storage and retrieval systems, electronic, mechanical, photocopy, recording, etc. without written permission from the copyright holder.

ISBN; 978-0-9979051-0-6

# Dedication

I dedicate this book to all you wonderful people.

# How To Use This Book

This is a 46 day journal that is focused on cultivating more happiness in your life!

1. First read the quote and get inspired. I like to use these for a daily focus.

2. Start to think about what activities make you happy. Example: taking a walk outside, petting your cat, eating a mango in the sun, etc.

3. At the end of your day, or whenever you notice it, jot down what went right. This is to help your mind learn to focus on the positive instead of the negative. Remember everything counts no matter how big or small.

4. The Happiness Meter is to track how happy you were today. Hopefully you will notice some patterns in time. Just shade in the meter. Super happy is like a 10 and It can only go up from here is like a 0.

5. Take some time to write what you are thankful for. Bringing in the element of gratitude can only bring you up, up, up!

6. Draw anything that made you smile today, paste in a magazine clipping, or pop in a goodie you found somewhere. It is up to you.

*The most important thing is to enjoy your life
- to be happy- it's all that matters.
Audrey Hepburn*

When I do this it makes me feel happy........

_____
_____
_____
_____
_____
_____
_____
_____
_____

I noticed this went right today.......

_____
_____
_____
_____
_____
_____
_____
_____
_____

*happiness meter*

date _____

super happy

I am so thankful for.......

_____
_____
_____
_____
_____
_____
_____
_____
_____
_____
_____
_____

It can only go up from here

*I saw something that made me smile*

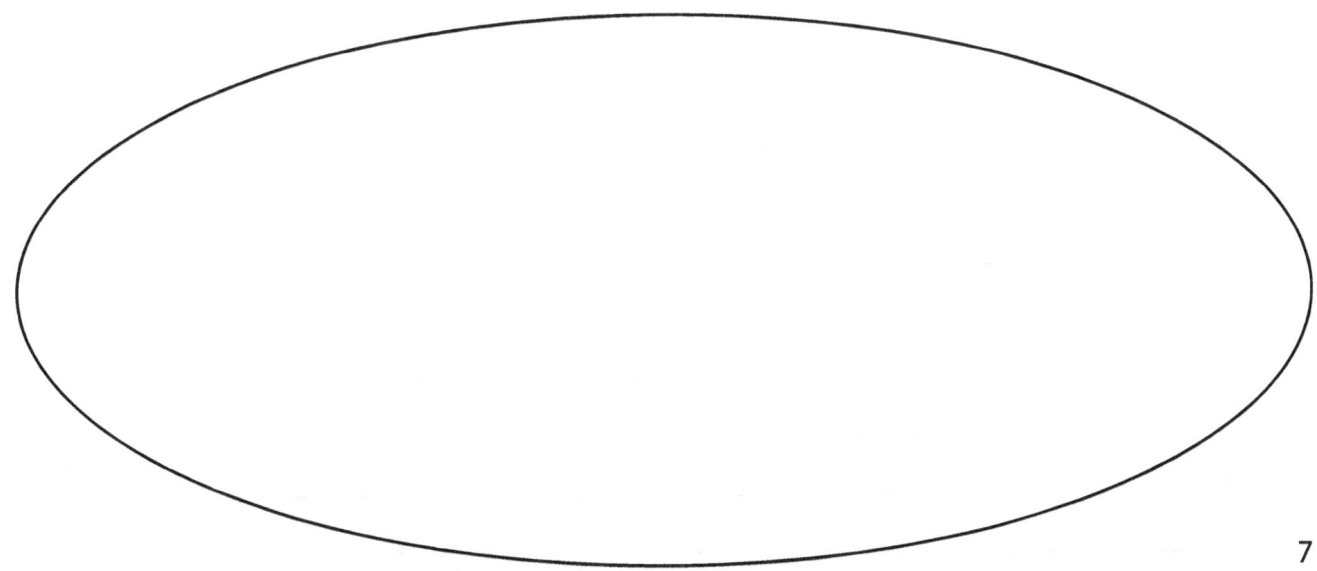

*I am determined to be cheerful and happy in whatever situation I may find myself. For I have learned that the greater part of our misery or unhappiness is determined not by our circumstance but by our disposition.*
*Martha Washington*

When I do this it makes me feel happy........

_____
_____
_____
_____
_____
_____
_____
_____
_____

I noticed this went right today.......

_____
_____
_____
_____
_____
_____
_____
_____
_____
_____

## happiness meter

date _____

super happy

# I am so thankful for.......

‗ ‗ ‗ ‗ ‗ ‗ ‗ ‗ ‗ ‗ ‗ ‗ ‗ ‗ ‗ ‗ ‗ ‗ ‗ ‗ ‗ ‗

‗ ‗ ‗ ‗ ‗ ‗ ‗ ‗ ‗ ‗ ‗ ‗ ‗ ‗ ‗ ‗ ‗ ‗ ‗ ‗ ‗ ‗

‗ ‗ ‗ ‗ ‗ ‗ ‗ ‗ ‗ ‗ ‗ ‗ ‗ ‗ ‗ ‗ ‗ ‗ ‗ ‗ ‗ ‗

‗ ‗ ‗ ‗ ‗ ‗ ‗ ‗ ‗ ‗ ‗ ‗ ‗ ‗ ‗ ‗ ‗ ‗ ‗ ‗ ‗ ‗

‗ ‗ ‗ ‗ ‗ ‗ ‗ ‗ ‗ ‗ ‗ ‗ ‗ ‗ ‗ ‗ ‗ ‗ ‗ ‗ ‗ ‗

‗ ‗ ‗ ‗ ‗ ‗ ‗ ‗ ‗ ‗ ‗ ‗ ‗ ‗ ‗ ‗ ‗ ‗ ‗ ‗ ‗ ‗

‗ ‗ ‗ ‗ ‗ ‗ ‗ ‗ ‗ ‗ ‗ ‗ ‗ ‗ ‗ ‗ ‗ ‗ ‗ ‗ ‗ ‗

‗ ‗ ‗ ‗ ‗ ‗ ‗ ‗ ‗ ‗ ‗ ‗ ‗ ‗ ‗ ‗ ‗ ‗ ‗ ‗ ‗ ‗

‗ ‗ ‗ ‗ ‗ ‗ ‗ ‗ ‗ ‗ ‗ ‗ ‗ ‗ ‗ ‗ ‗ ‗ ‗ ‗ ‗ ‗

It can only go up from here

*I saw something that made me smile*

*If you want to be happy, be.*
Leo Tolstoy

When I do this it makes me feel happy........

_____
_____
_____
_____
_____
_____
_____
_____

I noticed this went right today.......

_____
_____
_____
_____
_____
_____
_____
_____

*happiness meter*

date_____

super happy

## I am so thankful for.......

_____
_____
_____
_____
_____
_____
_____
_____
_____
_____
_____
_____

It can only go up from here

*I saw something that made me smile*

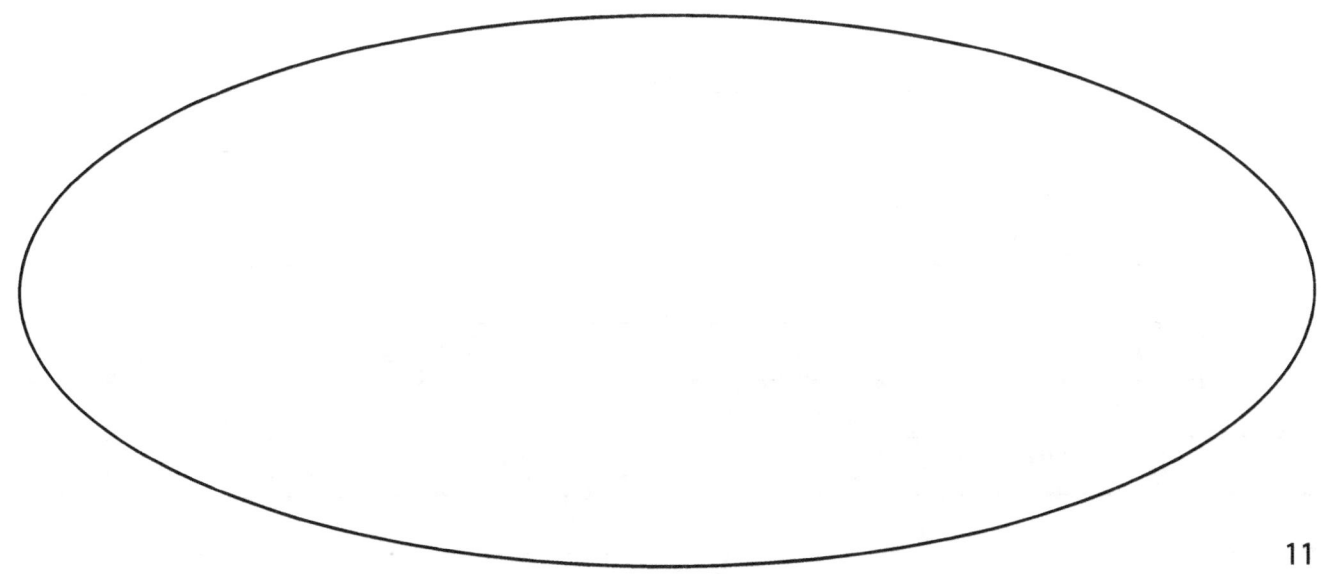

*The purpose of our lives is to be happy.*
*Dalai Lama*

When I do this it makes me feel happy........
___
___
___
___
___
___
___
___
___

I noticed this went right today.......
___
___
___
___
___
___
___
___
___

## *happiness meter*

date_____

super happy

## I am so thankful for.......

_____
_____
_____
_____
_____
_____
_____
_____
_____
_____
_____

It can only go up from here

## *I saw something that made me smile*

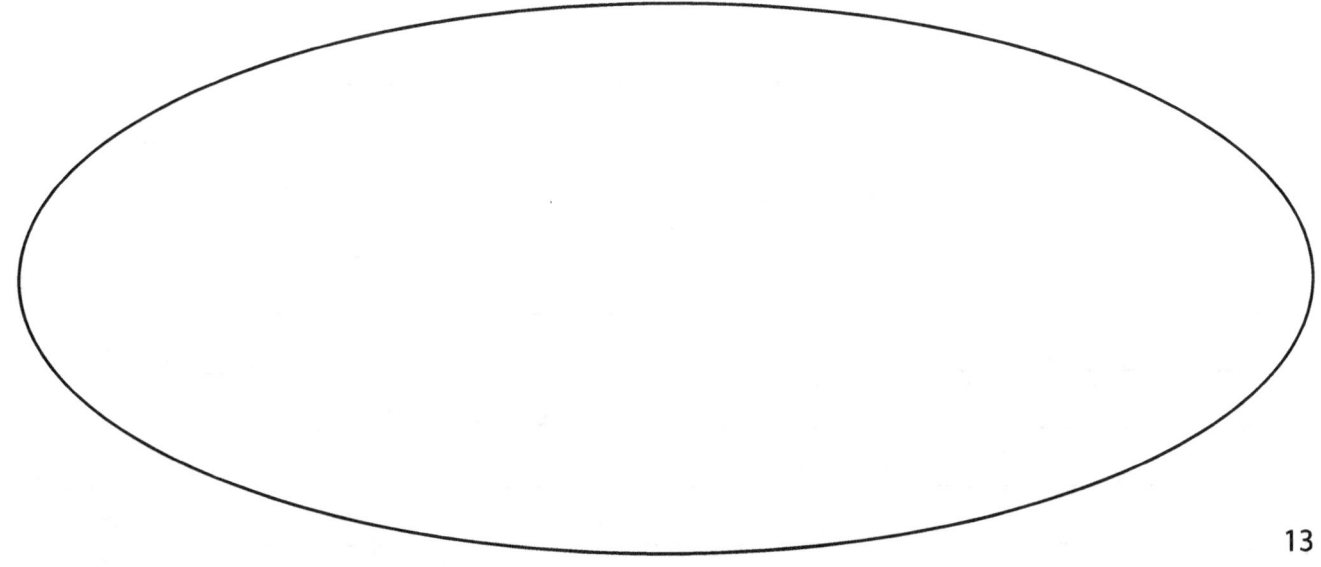

*Believe in yourself! Have faith in your abilities! Without a humble but reasonable confidence in your own powers you cannot be successful or happy.*
*Norman Vincent Peale*

When I do this it makes me feel happy........

_____
_____
_____
_____
_____
_____
_____
_____
_____
_____

I noticed this went right today.......

_____
_____
_____
_____
_____
_____
_____
_____
_____

## *happiness meter*

date_____

super happy

## I am so thankful for.......

_____
_____
_____
_____
_____
_____
_____
_____
_____
_____
_____
_____

It can only go up from here

## *I saw something that made me smile*

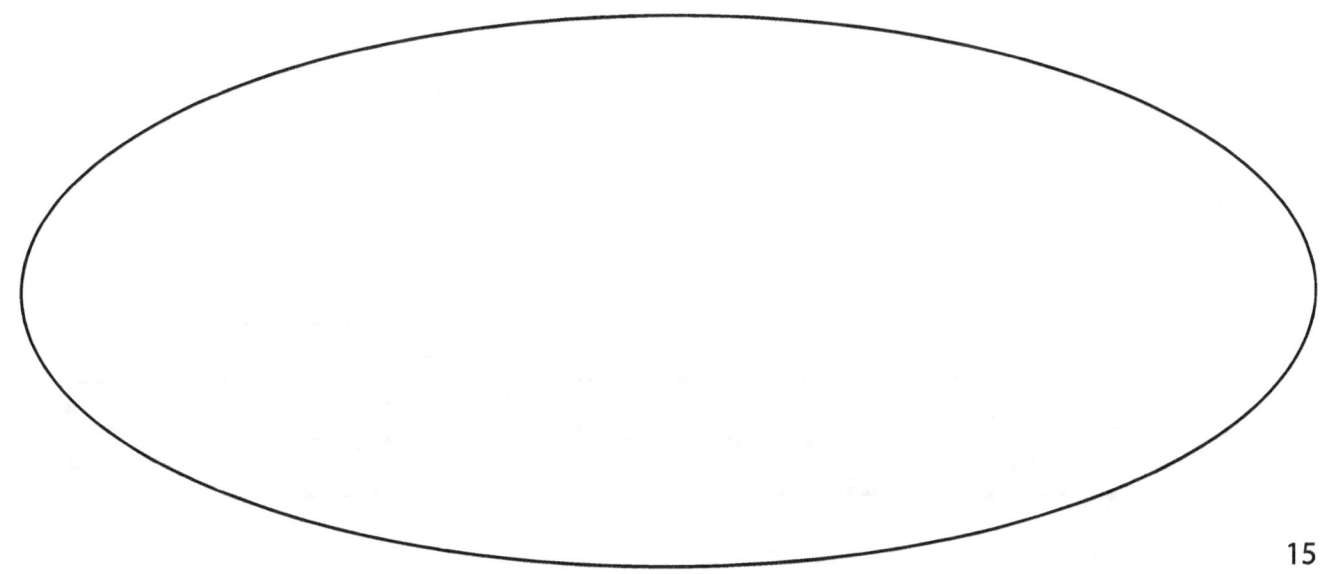

*Very little is needed to make a happy life; it is all within yourself, in your way of thinking.*
Marcus Aurelius

When I do this it makes me feel happy........

_____
_____
_____
_____
_____
_____
_____
_____
_____

I noticed this went right today.......

_____
_____
_____
_____
_____
_____
_____
_____
_____

# *happiness meter*

date_____

super happy

## I am so thankful for.......

_____
_____
_____
_____
_____
_____
_____
_____
_____
_____
_____

It can only go up from here

## *I saw something that made me smile*

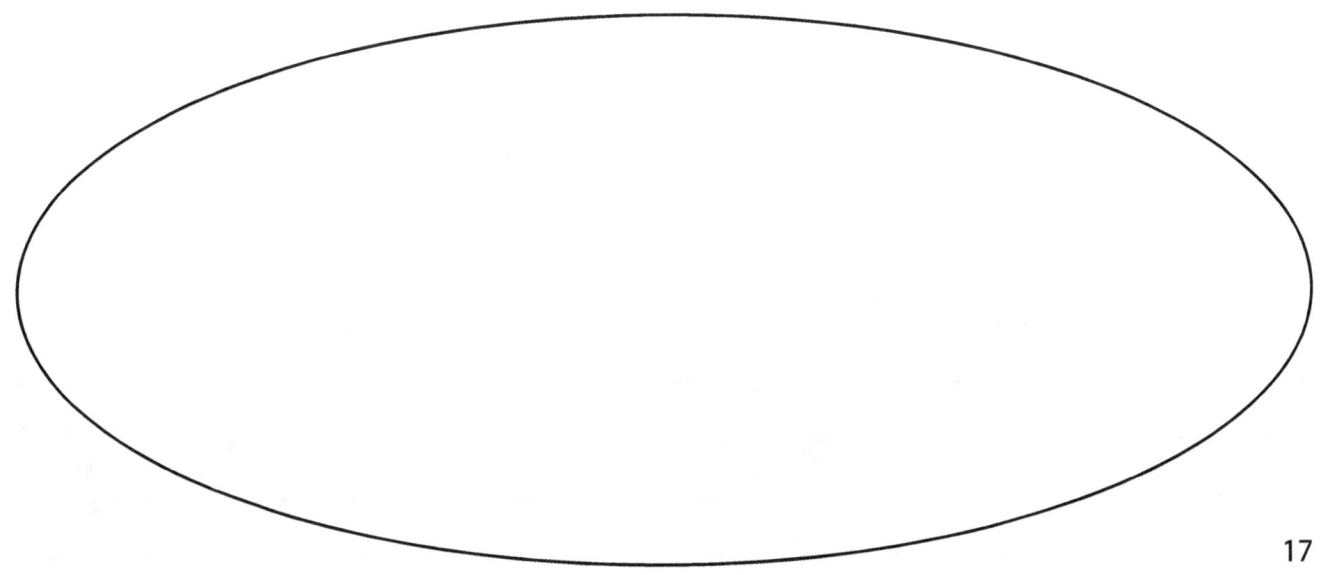

*Let us be grateful to people who make us happy, they are the charming gardeners who make our souls blossom.*
*Marcel Proust*

When I do this it makes me feel happy........

_____
_____
_____
_____
_____
_____
_____
_____
_____
_____

I noticed this went right today.......

_____
_____
_____
_____
_____
_____
_____
_____
_____

## *happiness meter*

super happy

date _____

I am so thankful for.......

_____
_____
_____
_____
_____
_____
_____
_____
_____
_____
_____

It can only go up from here

## *I saw something that made me smile*

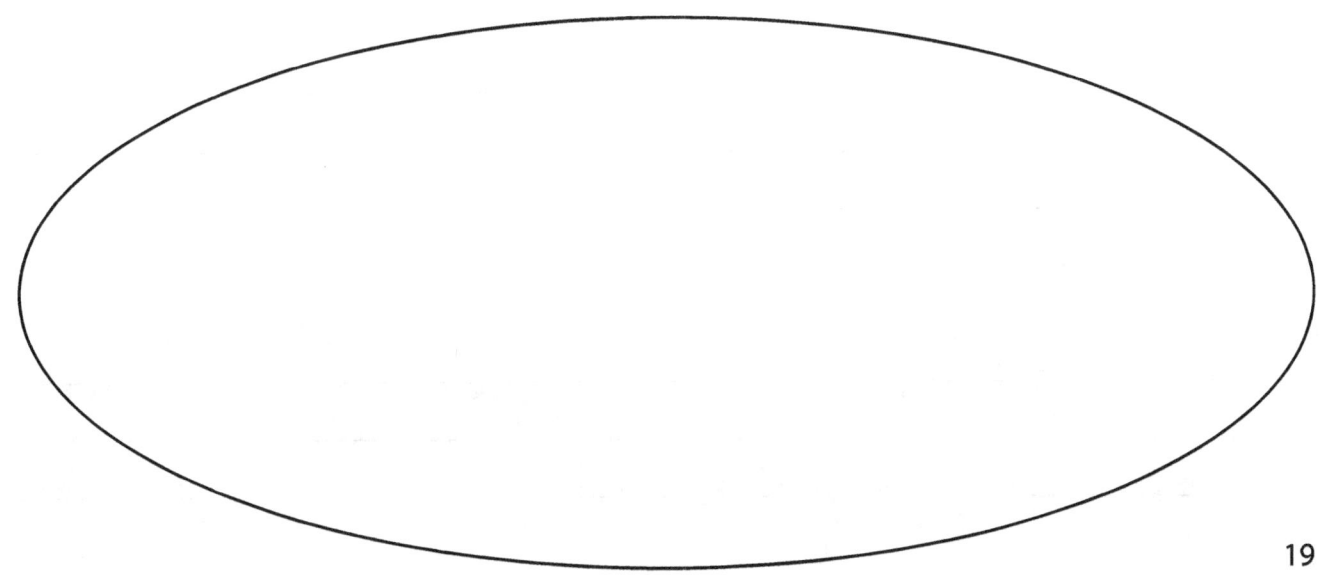

*Think of all the beauty still left around you and be happy.*
*Anne Frank*

When I do this it makes me feel happy........

_____
_____
_____
_____
_____
_____
_____
_____
_____

I noticed this went right today.......

_____
_____
_____
_____
_____
_____
_____
_____
_____
_____

*happiness meter*

date _____

super happy

I am so thankful for.......

_____
_____
_____
_____
_____
_____
_____
_____
_____
_____
_____

It can only go up from here

*I saw something that made me smile*

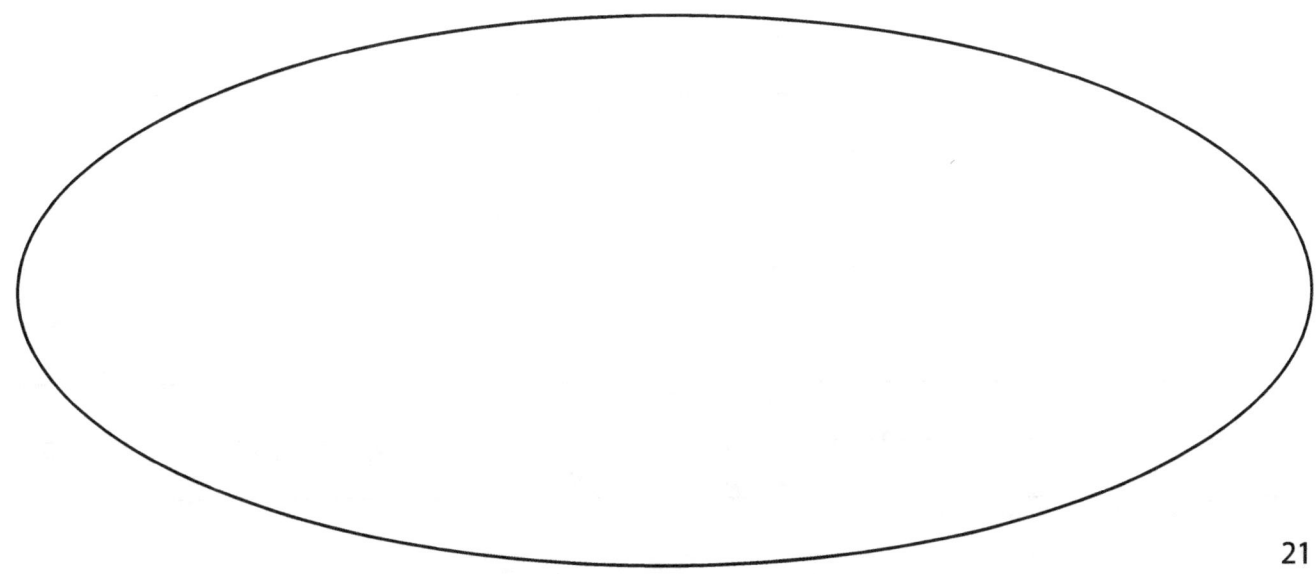

*Be happy with what you have and are, be generous with both,
and you won't have to hunt for happiness.*
*William E. Gladstone*

When I do this it makes me feel happy........

_____
_____
_____
_____
_____
_____
_____
_____
_____

I noticed this went right today.......

_____
_____
_____
_____
_____
_____
_____
_____

# *happiness meter*

date_____

super happy

## I am so thankful for.......

_____
_____
_____
_____
_____
_____
_____
_____
_____
_____
_____
_____

It can only go up from here

## *I saw something that made me smile*

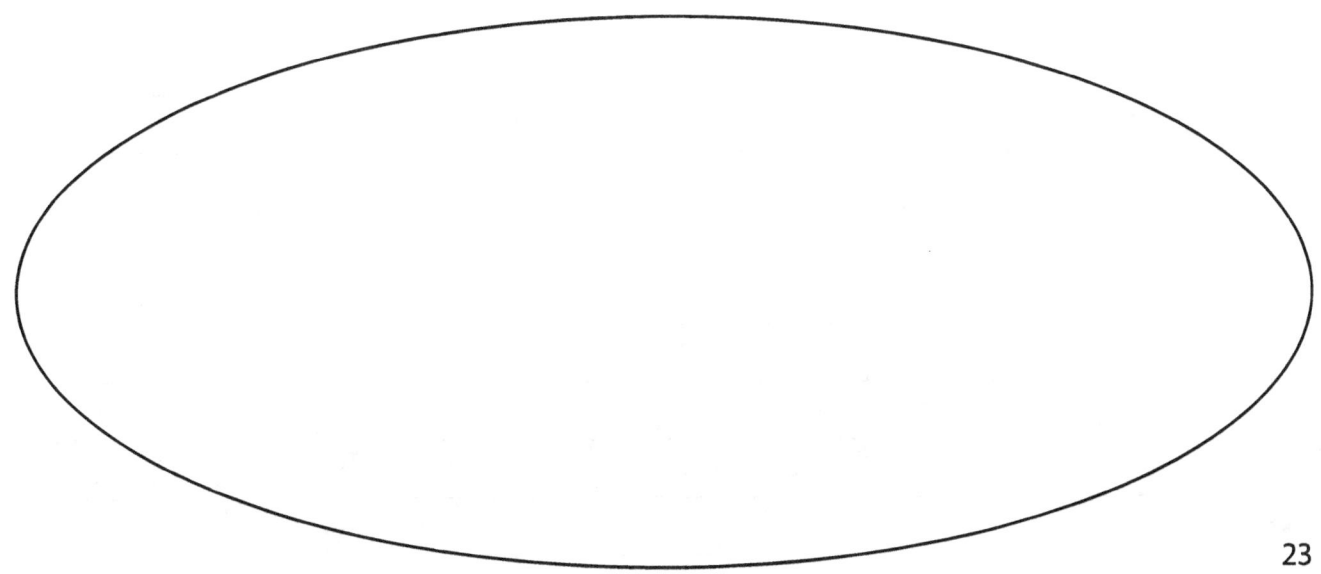

23

*It's easy to impress me. I don't need a fancy party to be happy. Just good friends, good food, and good laughs. I'm happy. I'm satisfied. I'm content.*
*Maria Sharapova*

When I do this it makes me feel happy........

---
---
---
---
---
---
---
---
---
---

I noticed this went right today.......

---
---
---
---
---
---
---
---
---
---

## *happiness meter*

super happy

date _____

## I am so thankful for.......

_____
_____
_____
_____
_____
_____
_____
_____
_____
_____
_____
_____

It can only go up from here

*I saw something that made me smile*

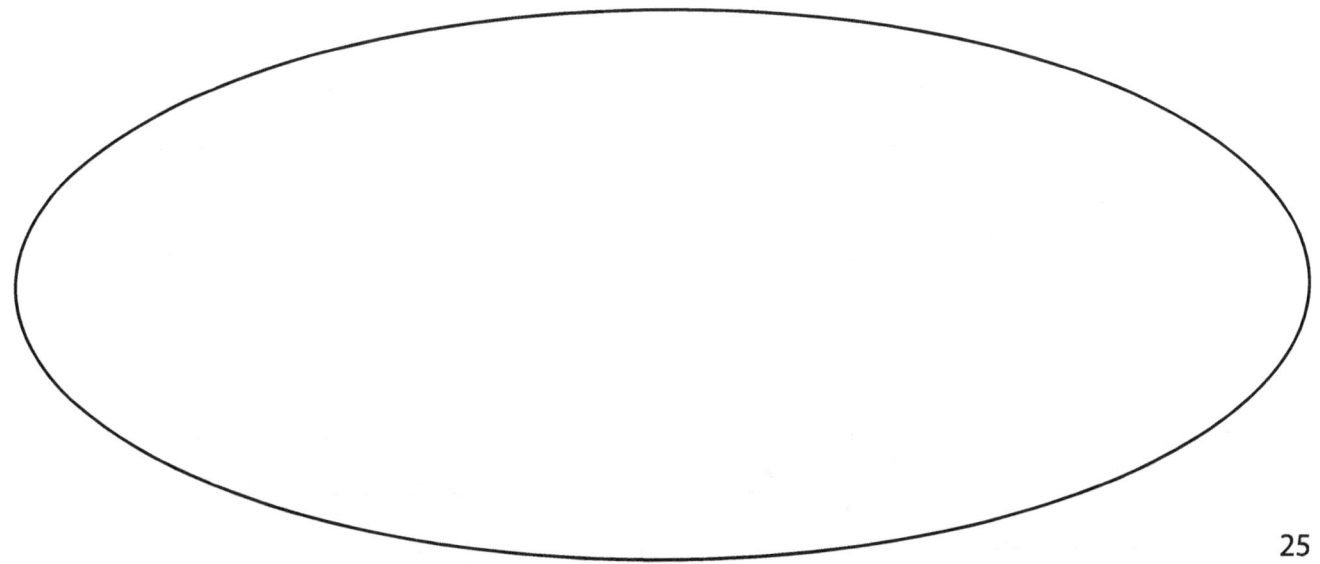

*There are lots of people I admire and respect, but I don't necessarily want to be like them. I'm too happy being myself.*
*James D'arcy*

When I do this it makes me feel happy........

_____
_____
_____
_____
_____
_____
_____
_____
_____

I noticed this went right today.......

_____
_____
_____
_____
_____
_____
_____
_____
_____

## *happiness meter*

date _____

super happy

## I am so thankful for.......

_____
_____
_____
_____
_____
_____
_____
_____
_____
_____
_____
_____

It can only go up from here

## *I saw something that made me smile*

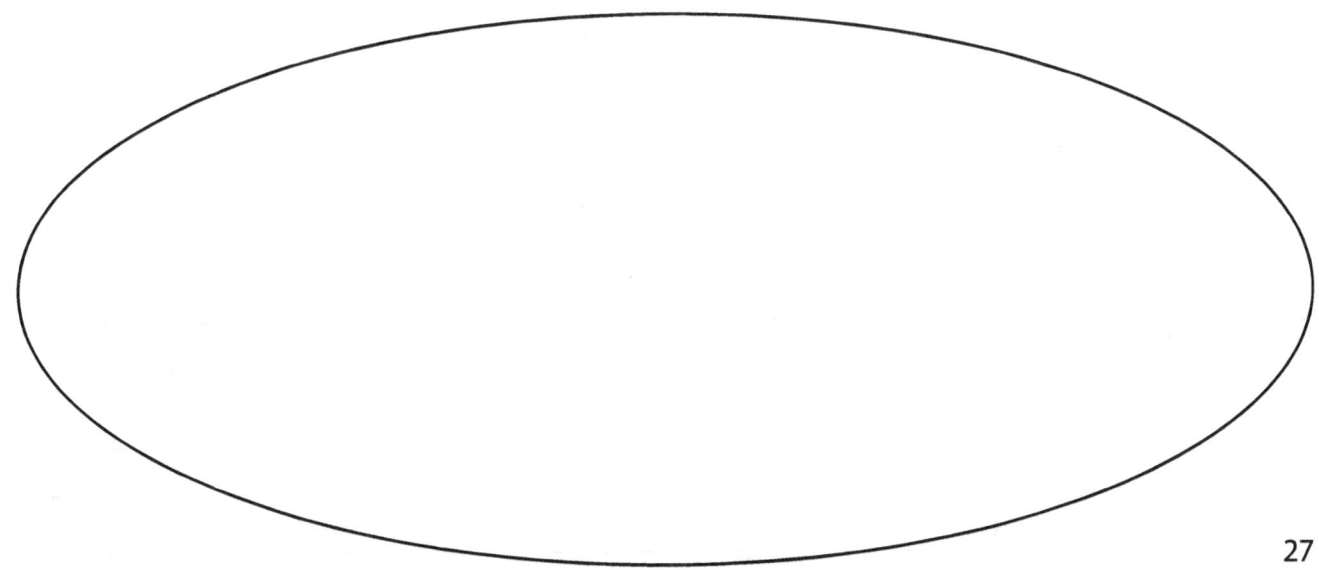

*A simple life is good with me. I don't need a whole lot. For me, a T-shirt, a pair of shorts, barefoot on a beach and I'm happy.*
*Yanni*

When I do this it makes me feel happy........

_____
_____
_____
_____
_____
_____
_____
_____
_____
_____

I noticed this went right today.......

_____
_____
_____
_____
_____
_____
_____
_____
_____

## *happiness meter*

date_____

super happy

# I am so thankful for.......

_____
_____
_____
_____
_____
_____
_____
_____
_____
_____
_____
_____

It can only go up from here

## *I saw something that made me smile*

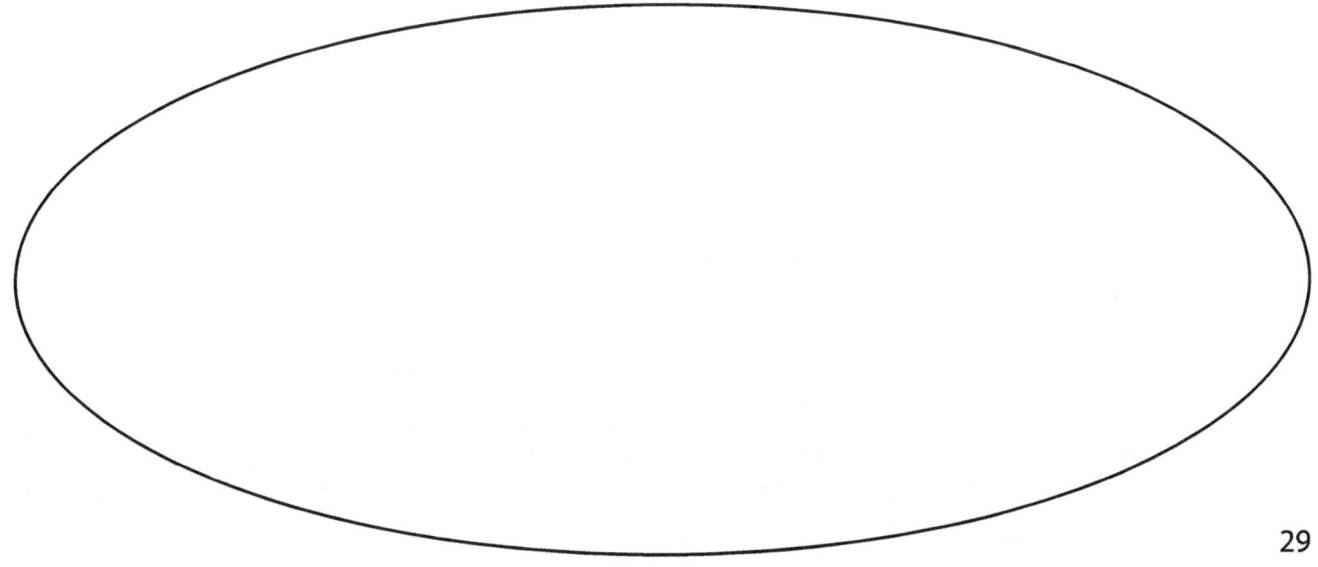

*The only thing that will make you happy is being happy with who you are, and not who people think you are.*
*Goldie Hawn*

When I do this it makes me feel happy........
_____
_____
_____
_____
_____
_____
_____
_____
_____

I noticed this went right today.......
_____
_____
_____
_____
_____
_____
_____
_____
_____

*happiness meter*

date_____

super happy

## I am so thankful for.......

_____
_____
_____
_____
_____
_____
_____
_____
_____
_____
_____

It can only go up from here

## *I saw something that made me smile*

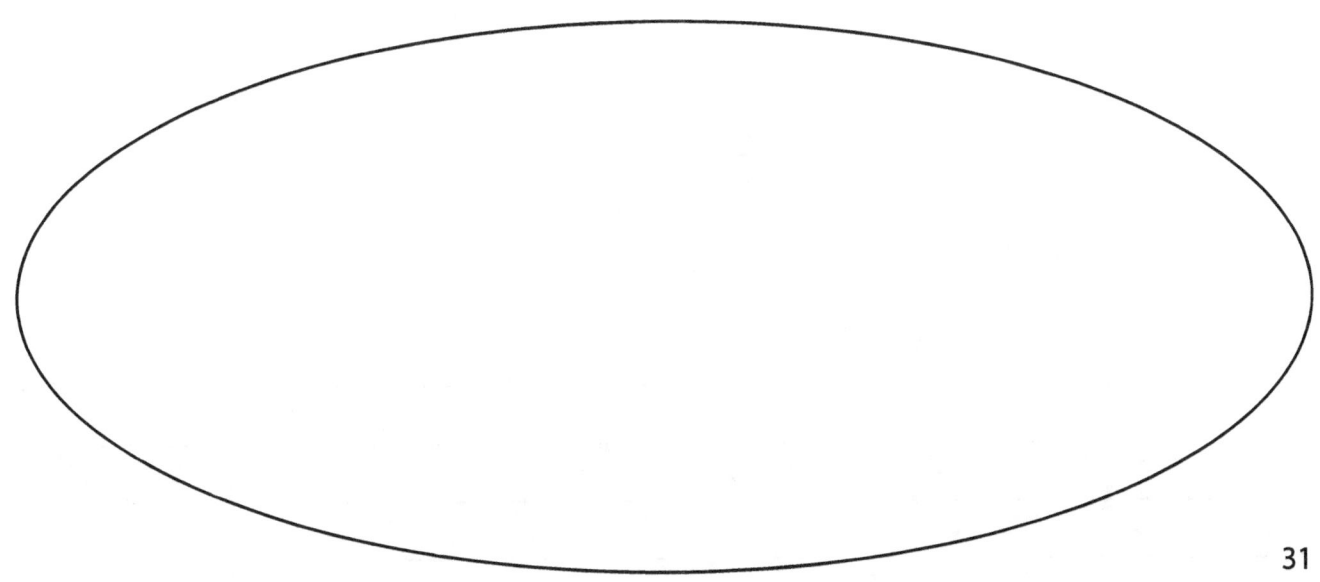

*Trust yourself. Create the kind of self that you will be happy to live with all your life. Make the most of yourself by fanning the tiny, inner sparks of possibility into flames of achievement.*
*Golda Meir*

When I do this it makes me feel happy........

_____
_____
_____
_____
_____
_____
_____
_____
_____

I noticed this went right today.......

_____
_____
_____
_____
_____
_____
_____
_____
_____

## *happiness meter*

date _____

super happy

# I am so thankful for.......

_____
_____
_____
_____
_____
_____
_____
_____
_____
_____
_____
_____

It can only go up from here

## *I saw something that made me smile*

*Most folks are as happy as they make up their minds to be.*
*Abraham Lincoln*

When I do this it makes me feel happy........

___

I noticed this went right today.......

*happiness meter*

super happy

date_____

I am so thankful for.......

_____
_____
_____
_____
_____
_____
_____
_____
_____
_____
_____
_____

It can only go up from here

*I saw something that made me smile*

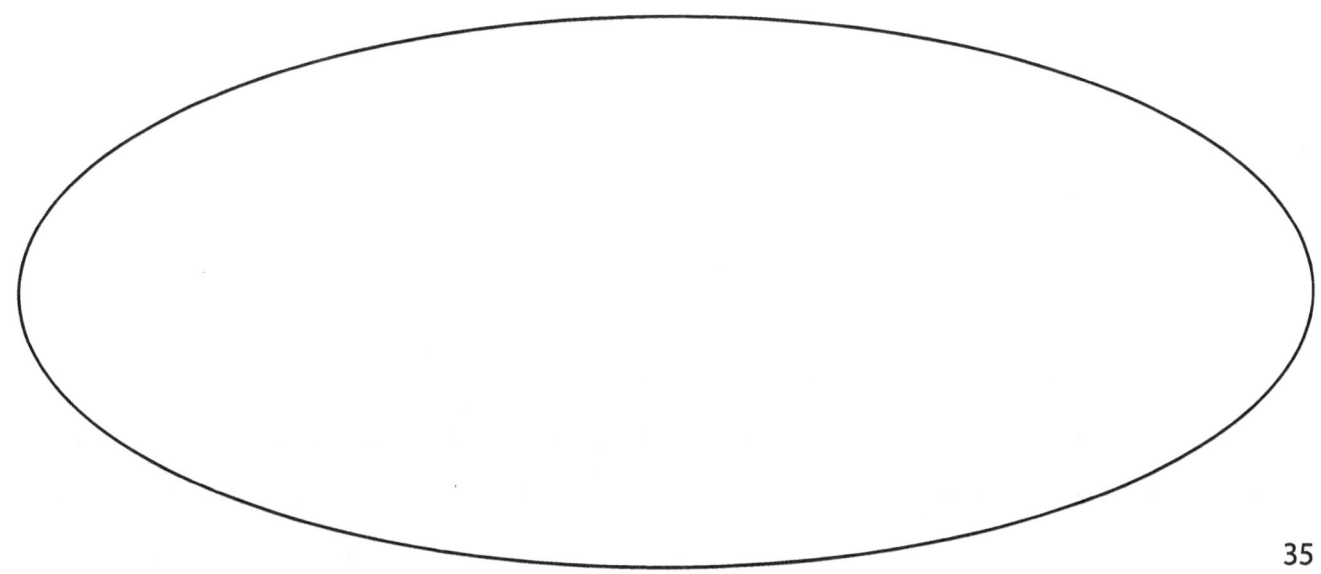

*Being in control of your life and having realistic expectations about your day-to-day challenges are the keys to stress management, which is perhaps the most important ingredient to living a happy, healthy and rewarding life.*
*Marilu Henner*

When I do this it makes me feel happy........

_____
_____
_____
_____
_____
_____
_____
_____
_____

I noticed this went right today.......

_____
_____
_____
_____
_____
_____
_____
_____
_____

## *happiness meter*

date_____

super happy

## I am so thankful for.......

_____
_____
_____
_____
_____
_____
_____
_____
_____
_____
_____

It can only go up from here

## *I saw something that made me smile*

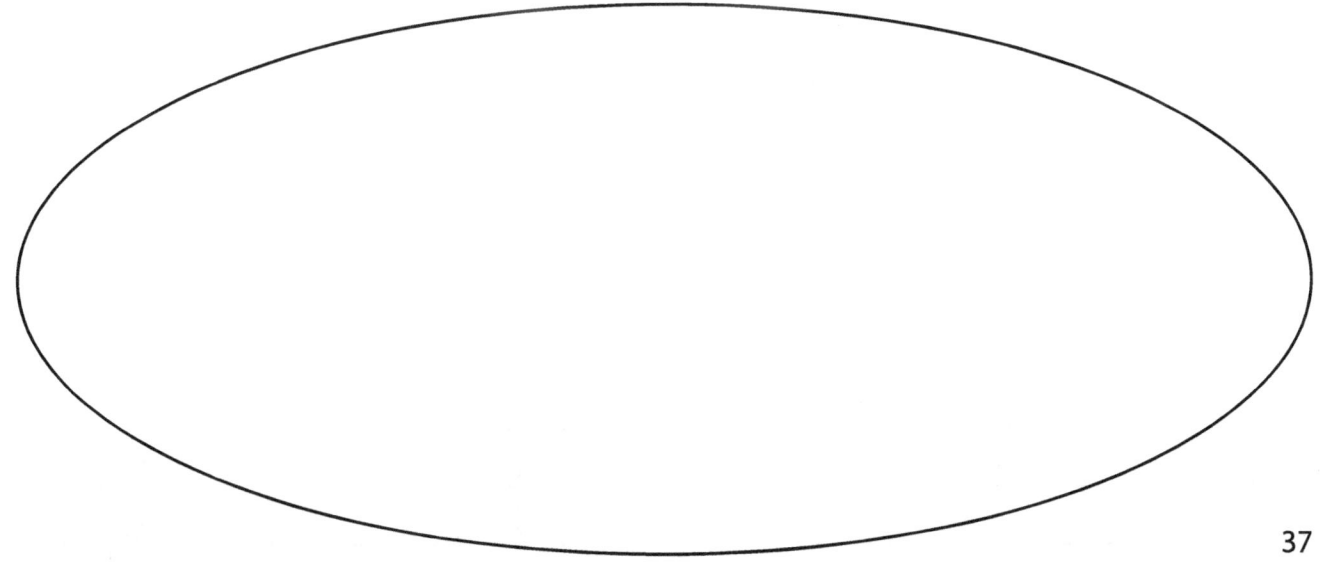

*If you can learn to love yourself and all the flaws, you can love other people so much better. And that makes you so happy.*
*Kristin Chenoweth*

When I do this it makes me feel happy……..

_____
_____
_____
_____
_____
_____
_____
_____
_____

I noticed this went right today…….

_____
_____
_____
_____
_____
_____
_____
_____
_____
_____

## *happiness meter*

date_____

super happy

## I am so thankful for.......

_____
_____
_____
_____
_____
_____
_____
_____
_____
_____
_____
_____

It can only go up from here

## *I saw something that made me smile*

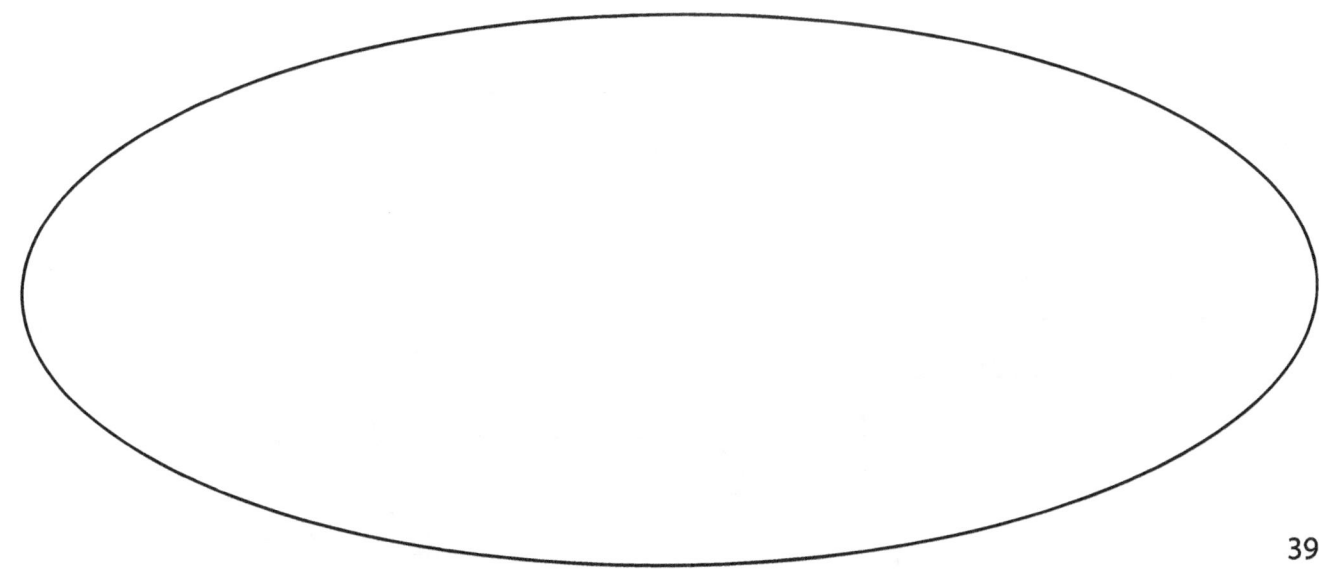

*Whoever is happy will make others happy too.*
*Anne Frank*

When I do this it makes me feel happy........

_____
_____
_____
_____
_____
_____
_____
_____

I noticed this went right today.......

_____
_____
_____
_____
_____
_____
_____
_____

## *happiness meter*

super happy

date _____

## I am so thankful for.......

_____
_____
_____
_____
_____
_____
_____
_____
_____
_____
_____

It can only go up from here

*I saw something that made me smile*

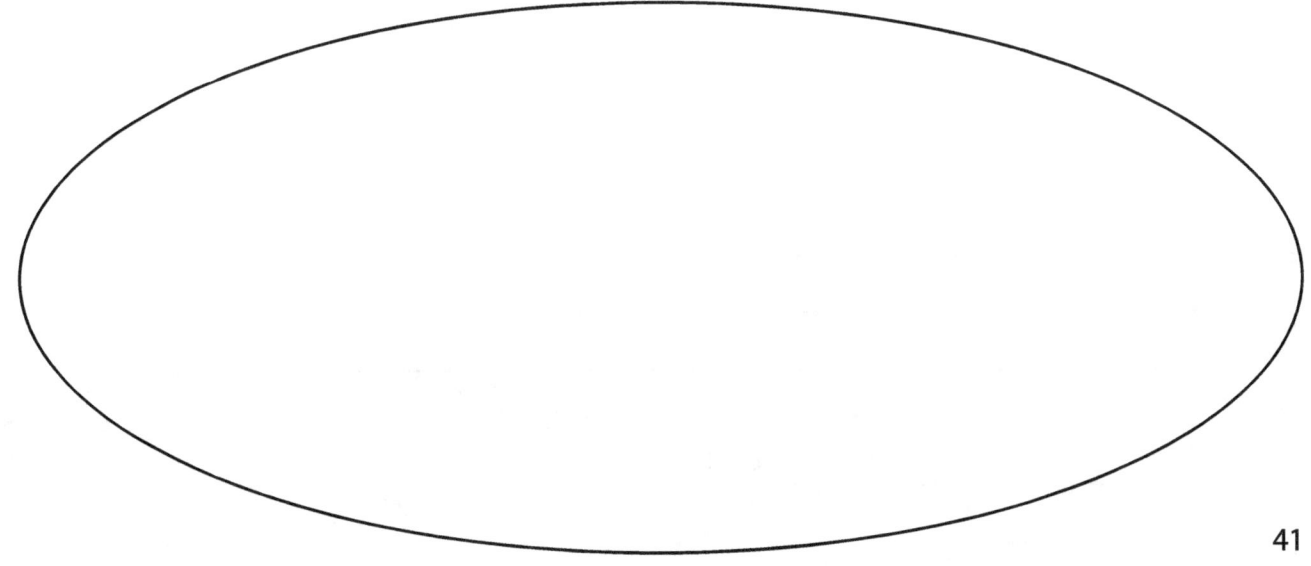

*Life is like a roller coaster, live it,
be happy, enjoy life.*
*Avril Lavigne*

When I do this it makes me feel happy……..

_____
_____
_____
_____
_____
_____
_____
_____
_____

I noticed this went right today…….

_____
_____
_____
_____
_____
_____
_____
_____
_____
_____

## *happiness meter*

date_____

super happy

## I am so thankful for.......

_____
_____
_____
_____
_____
_____
_____
_____
_____
_____
_____
_____

It can only go up from here

*I saw something that made me smile*

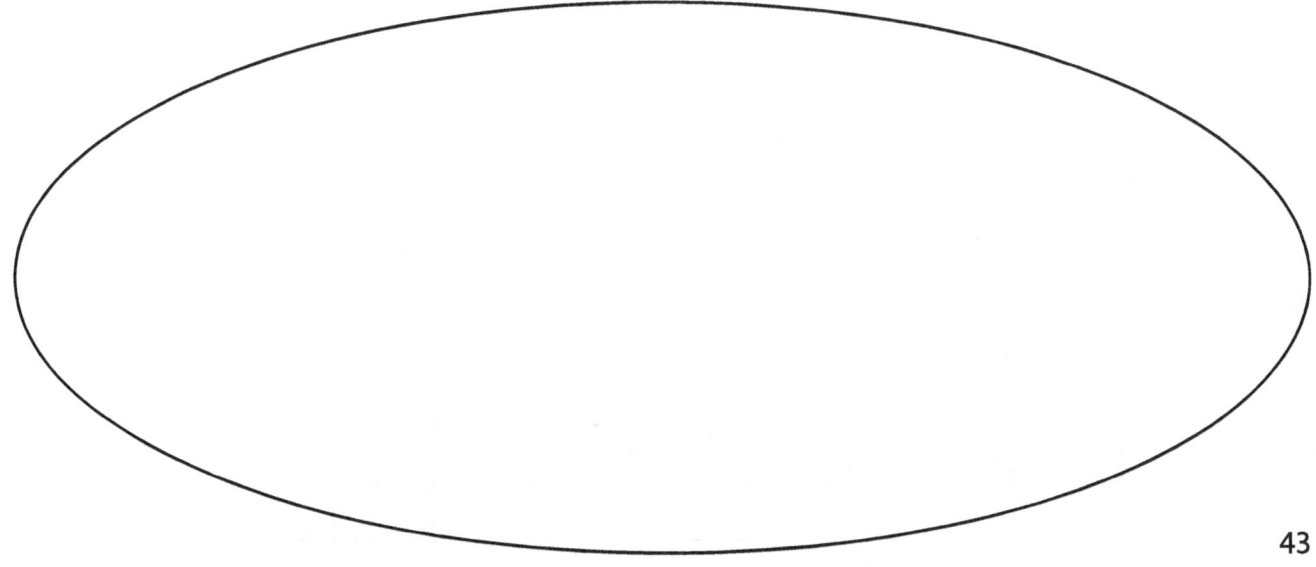

*You know, all that really matters is that
the people you love are happy and healthy.
Everything else is just sprinkles on the sundae.
Paul Walker*

When I do this it makes me feel happy........

_____
_____
_____
_____
_____
_____
_____
_____
_____

I noticed this went right today.......

_____
_____
_____
_____
_____
_____
_____
_____
_____
_____

## *happiness meter*

date ........................

super happy

I am so thankful for .......

_____
_____
_____
_____
_____
_____
_____
_____
_____
_____
_____

It can only go up from here

## *I saw something that made me smile*

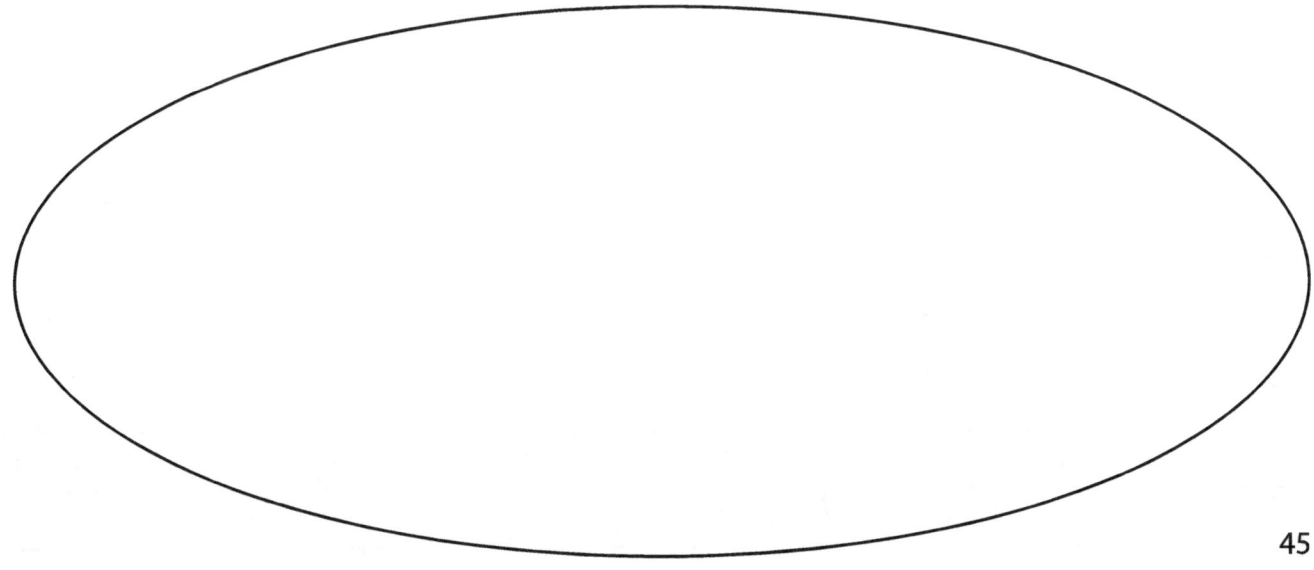

*If you want a happy ending, that depends, of course, on where you stop your story.*
*Orson Welles*

When I do this it makes me feel happy........

___

I noticed this went right today.......

## happiness meter

date_____

super happy

### I am so thankful for.......

_____
_____
_____
_____
_____
_____
_____
_____
_____
_____
_____
_____

It can only go up from here

*I saw something that made me smile*

*My theory on life is that life is beautiful. Life doesn't change. You have a day, and a night, and a month, and a year. We people change - we can be miserable or we can be happy. It's what you make of your life.*
*Mohammed bin Rashid Al Maktoum*

When I do this it makes me feel happy........

_____
_____
_____
_____
_____
_____
_____
_____
_____
_____

I noticed this went right today.......

_____
_____
_____
_____
_____
_____
_____
_____
_____

# *happiness meter*

date _____

super happy

## I am so thankful for.......

_____
_____
_____
_____
_____
_____
_____
_____
_____
_____
_____

It can only go up from here

## *I saw something that made me smile*

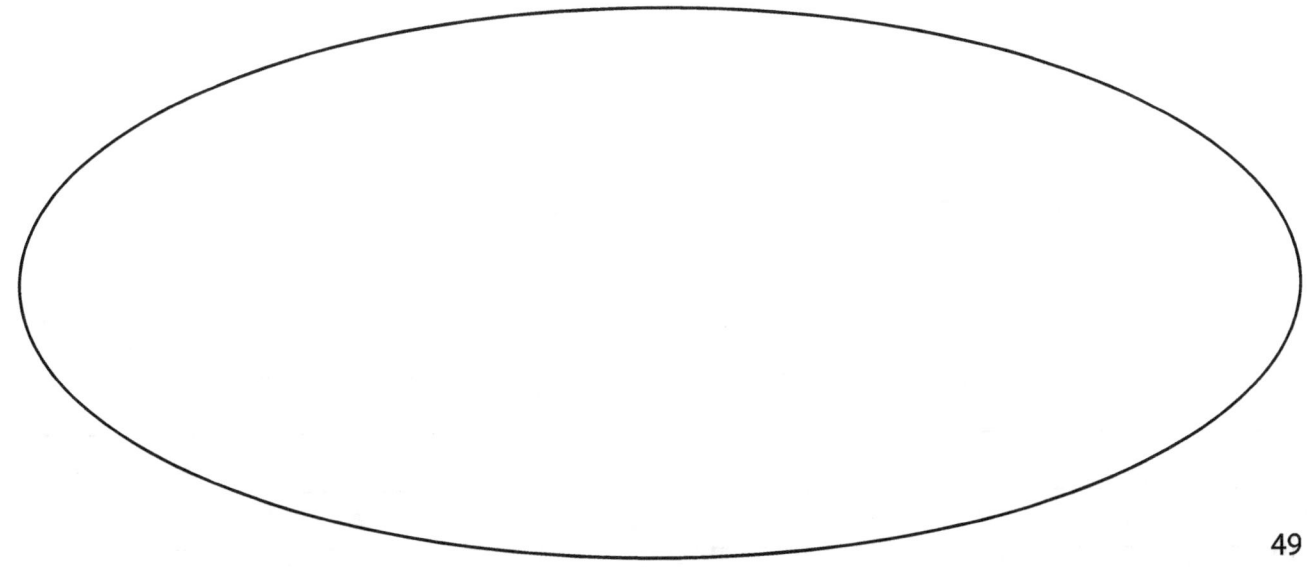

*I, not events, have the power to make me happy or unhappy today. I can choose which it shall be. Yesterday is dead, tomorrow hasn't arrived yet. I have just one day, today, and I'm going to be happy in it.*
*Groucho Marx*

When I do this it makes me feel happy........

_____
_____
_____
_____
_____
_____
_____
_____
_____

I noticed this went right today.......

_____
_____
_____
_____
_____
_____
_____
_____
_____
_____

## *happiness meter*

date _____

super happy

## I am so thankful for.......

_____
_____
_____
_____
_____
_____
_____
_____
_____
_____
_____

It can only go up from here

## *I saw something that made me smile*

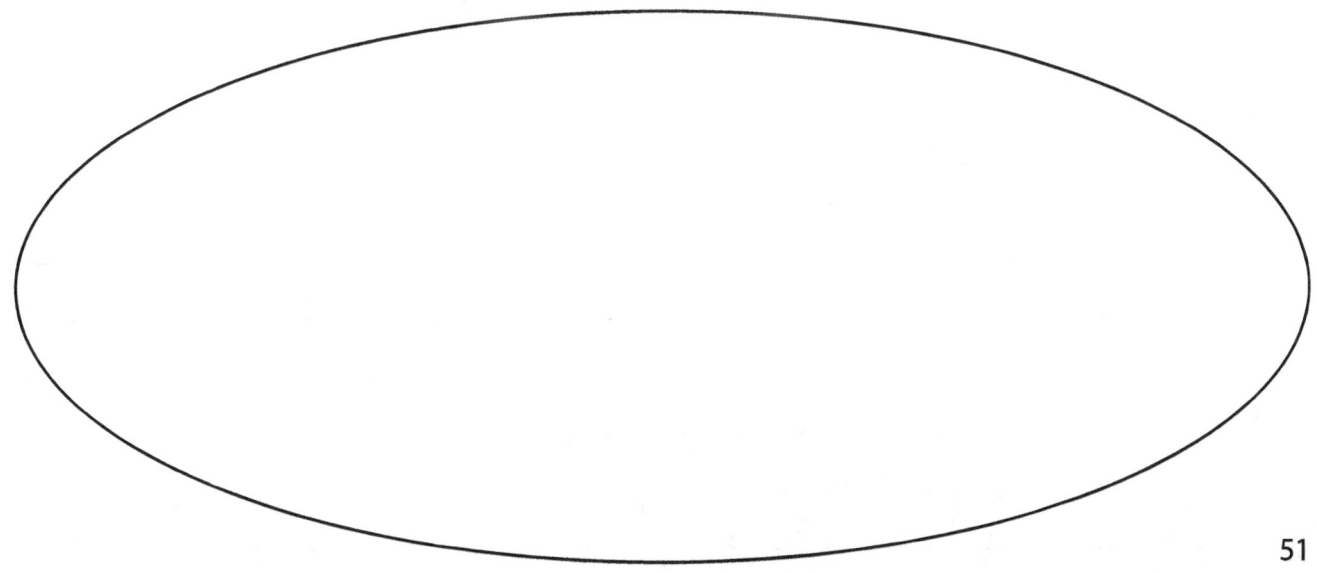

*It's all about quality of life and finding a happy balance between work and friends and family.*
*Philip Green*

When I do this it makes me feel happy........

_____
_____
_____
_____
_____
_____
_____
_____

I noticed this went right today.......

_____
_____
_____
_____
_____
_____
_____
_____

## *happiness meter*

date _____

super happy

## I am so thankful for.......

_____
_____
_____
_____
_____
_____
_____
_____
_____
_____
_____

It can only go up from here

## *I saw something that made me smile*

*To be happy, it first takes being comfortable being in your own shoes. The rest can work up from there.*
*Sophia Bush*

When I do this it makes me feel happy........

_____
_____
_____
_____
_____
_____
_____
_____
_____

I noticed this went right today.......

_____
_____
_____
_____
_____
_____
_____
_____
_____

## *happiness meter*

super happy

It can only go up from here

date _____

## I am so thankful for.......

_____
_____
_____
_____
_____
_____
_____
_____
_____
_____
_____

*I saw something that made me smile*

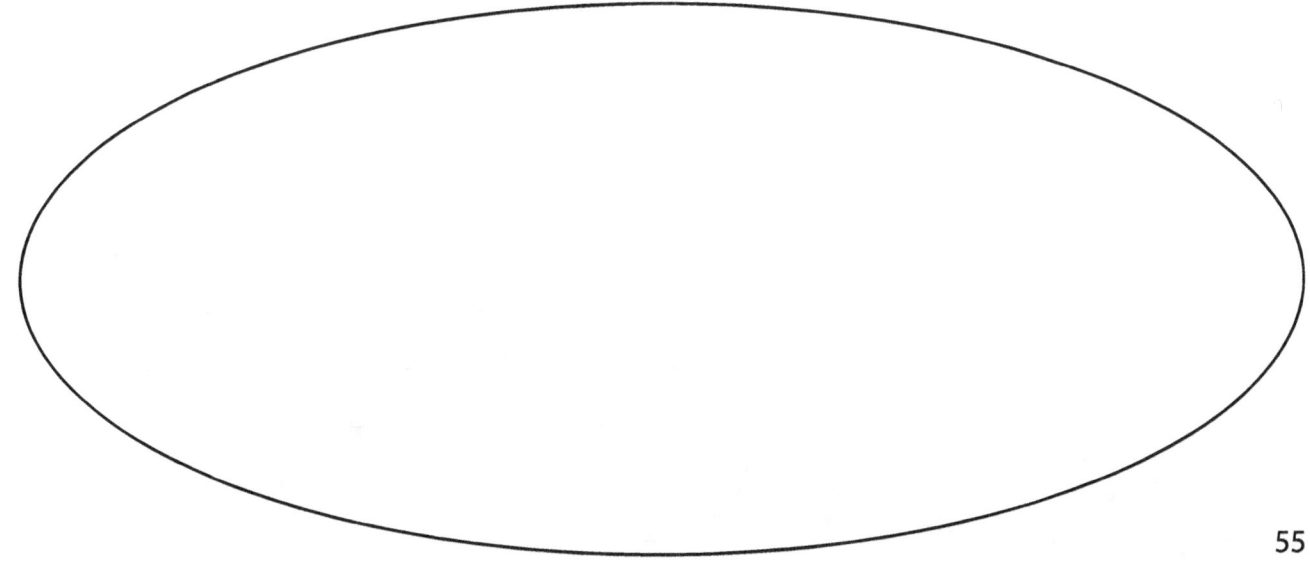

*I don't let anyone's insecurities, emotions, or opinions bother me. I know that if I am happy, that's all that matters to me.*
*Demi Lovato*

When I do this it makes me feel happy........

___

I noticed this went right today.......

*happiness meter*

date _____

super happy

I am so thankful for.......

_____
_____
_____
_____
_____
_____
_____
_____
_____
_____
_____

It can only go up from here

*I saw something that made me smile*

*Negative emotions like loneliness, envy, and guilt have an important role to play in a happy life; they're big, flashing signs that something needs to change.*
*Gretchen Rubin*

When I do this it makes me feel happy........

___

I noticed this went right today.......

# *happiness meter*

date_____

super happy

## I am so thankful for.......

_____
_____
_____
_____
_____
_____
_____
_____
_____
_____
_____
_____
_____

It can only go up from here

## *I saw something that made me smile*

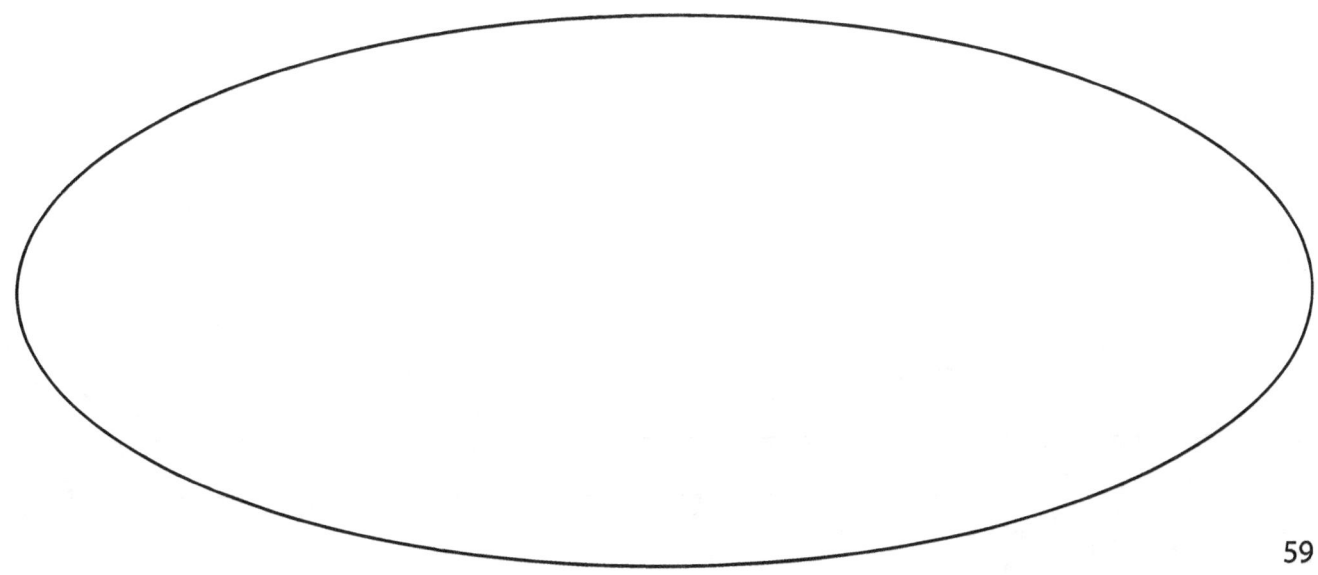

*Anyone's life truly lived consists of work, sunshine, exercise, soap, plenty of fresh air, and a happy contented spirit.*
*Lillie Langtry*

When I do this it makes me feel happy........

_____
_____
_____
_____
_____
_____
_____
_____

I noticed this went right today.......

_____
_____
_____
_____
_____
_____
_____
_____

## *happiness meter*

date _____

super happy

## I am so thankful for.......

_____
_____
_____
_____
_____
_____
_____
_____
_____
_____
_____

It can only go up from here

## *I saw something that made me smile*

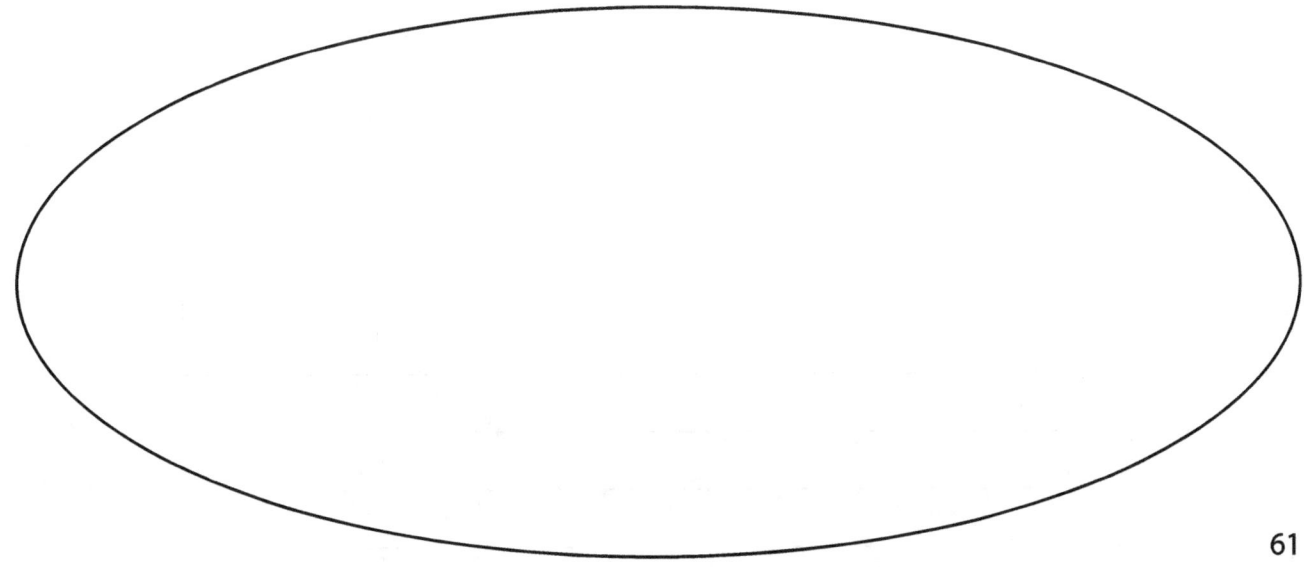

*Happiness is a choice. You can choose to be happy. There's going to be stress in life, but it's your choice whether you let it affect you or not.*
*Valerie Bertinelli*

When I do this it makes me feel happy........

_____
_____
_____
_____
_____
_____
_____
_____
_____

I noticed this went right today.......

_____
_____
_____
_____
_____
_____
_____
_____
_____

*happiness meter*

date_____

super happy

# I am so thankful for.......

_____
_____
_____
_____
_____
_____
_____
_____
_____
_____
_____

It can only go up from here

## *I saw something that made me smile*

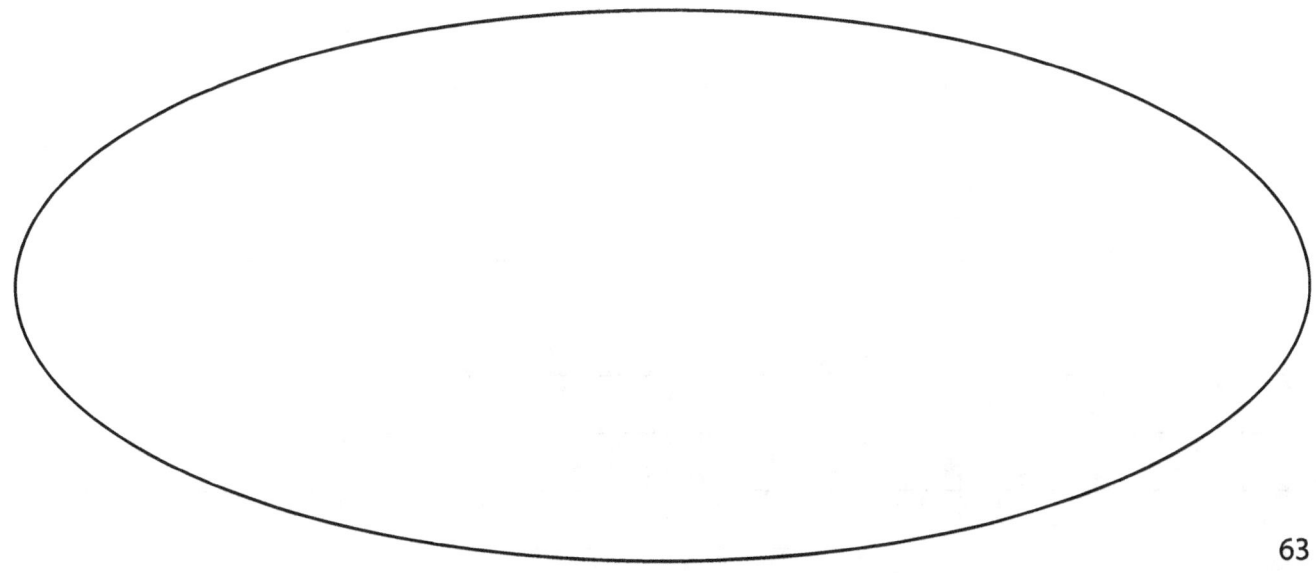

*Too often in life, something happens and we blame other people for us not being happy or satisfied or fulfilled. So the point is, we all have choices, and we make the choice to accept people or situations or to not accept situations.*
*Tom Brady*

When I do this it makes me feel happy........

_____
_____
_____
_____
_____
_____
_____
_____
_____

I noticed this went right today.......

_____
_____
_____
_____
_____
_____
_____
_____
_____

## *happiness meter*

date ........................

super happy

## I am so thankful for.......

_____
_____
_____
_____
_____
_____
_____
_____
_____
_____
_____

It can only go up from here

## *I saw something that made me smile*

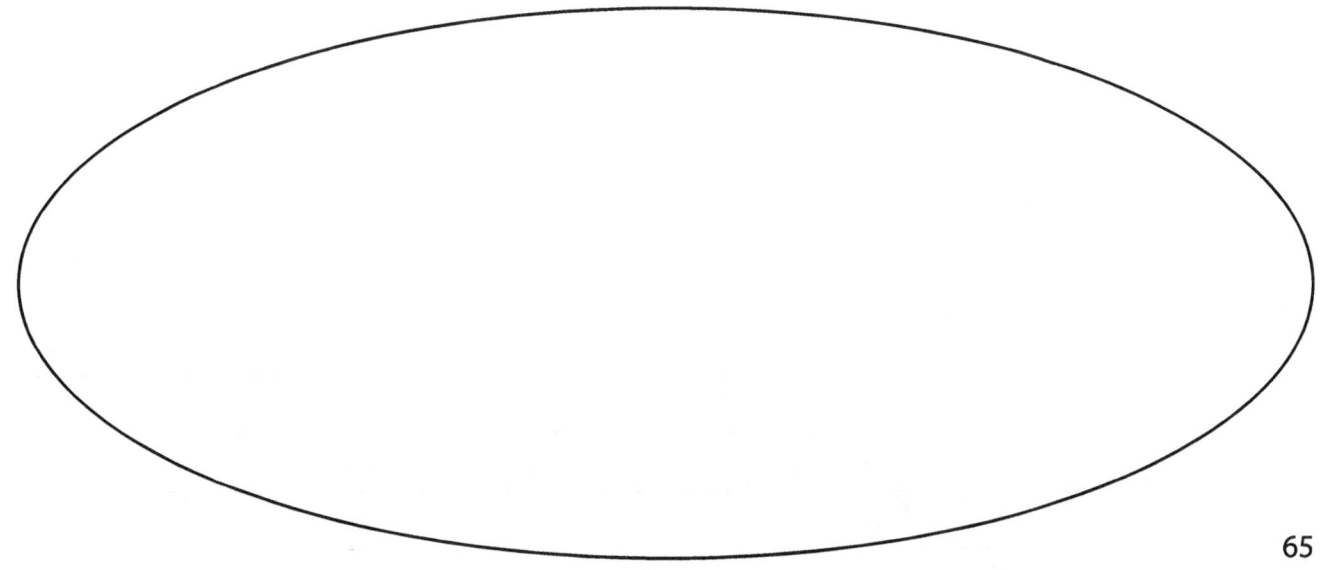

*Now and then it's good to pause in our pursuit of happiness and just be happy.*
*Guillaume Apollinaire*

When I do this it makes me feel happy……..

_____
_____
_____
_____
_____
_____
_____
_____
_____

I noticed this went right today…….

_____
_____
_____
_____
_____
_____
_____
_____
_____
_____

# *happiness meter*

date _____

super happy

## I am so thankful for.......

_____
_____
_____
_____
_____
_____
_____
_____
_____
_____
_____
_____

It can only go up from here

## *I saw something that made me smile*

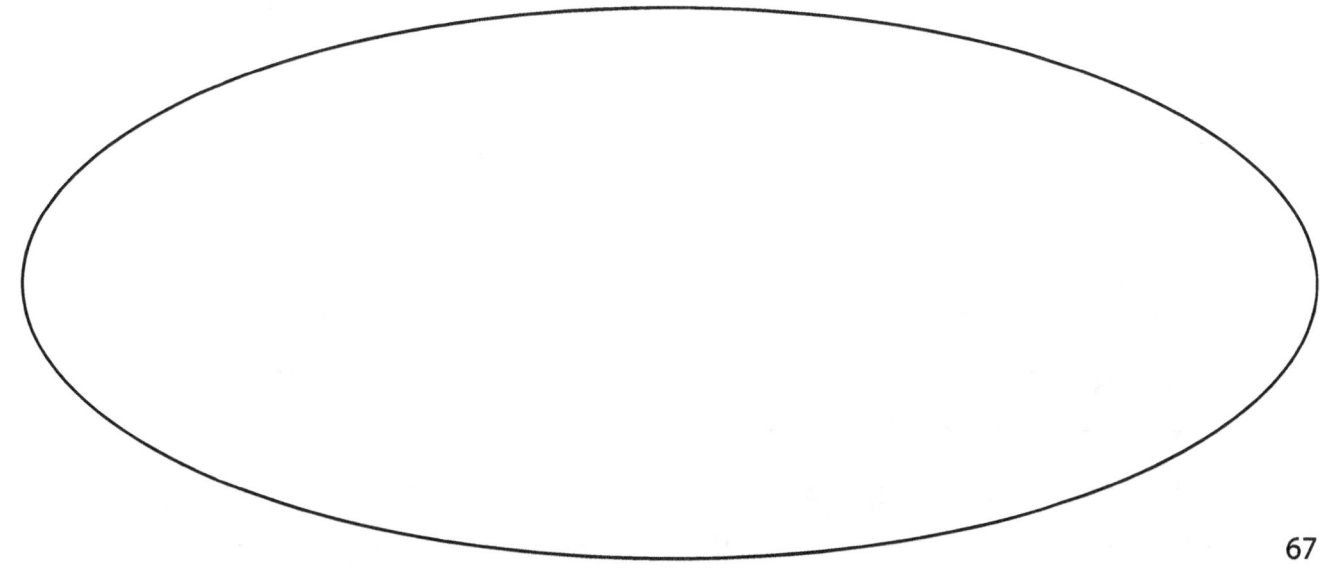

*With me, what you see is what you get. Yes, call me naive, but I love life. I am happy, and for that, I make no apologies. I do like to see the best in people, and when someone is nice to my face, I tend to believe them.*
*Joyce Giraud*

When I do this it makes me feel happy……..

_____
_____
_____
_____
_____
_____
_____
_____
_____

I noticed this went right today…….

_____
_____
_____
_____
_____
_____
_____
_____
_____

## *happiness meter*

date_____

super happy

# I am so thankful for.......

_____
_____
_____
_____
_____
_____
_____
_____
_____
_____
_____

It can only go up from here

## *I saw something that made me smile*

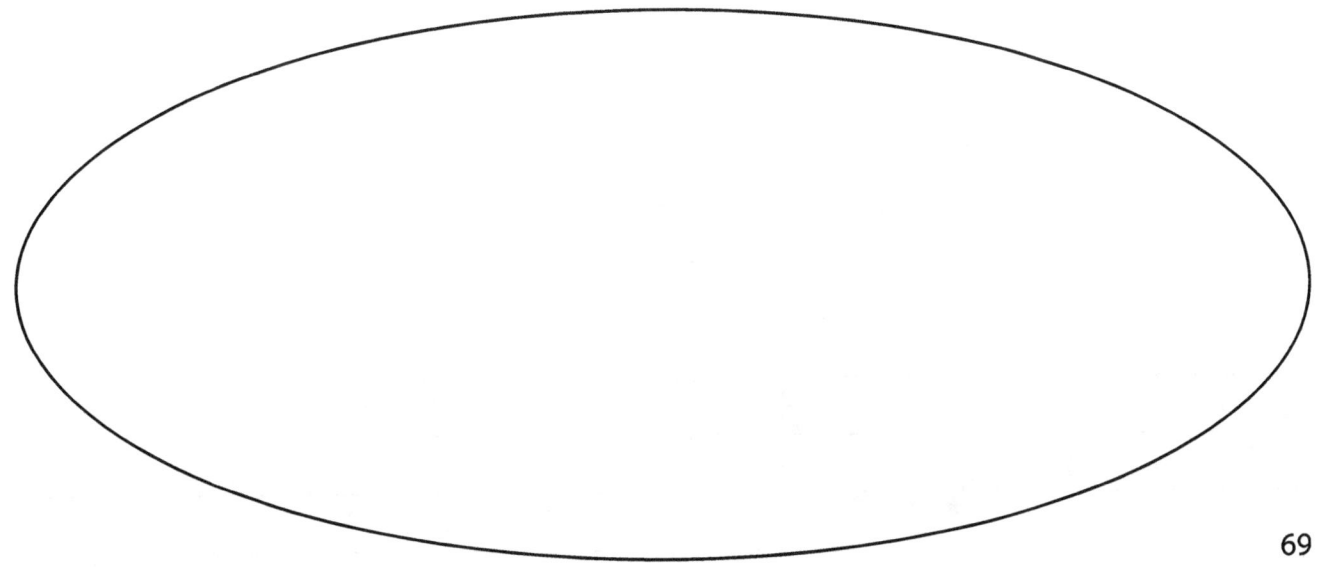

*Be happy with being you. Love your flaws. Own your quirks. And know that you are just as perfect as anyone else, exactly as you are.*
*Ariana Grande*

When I do this it makes me feel happy……..

_____
_____
_____
_____
_____
_____
_____
_____

I noticed this went right today…….

_____
_____
_____
_____
_____
_____
_____
_____

## *happiness meter*

date_____

super happy

## I am so thankful for.......

_____
_____
_____
_____
_____
_____
_____
_____
_____
_____
_____

It can only go up from here

### *I saw something that made me smile*

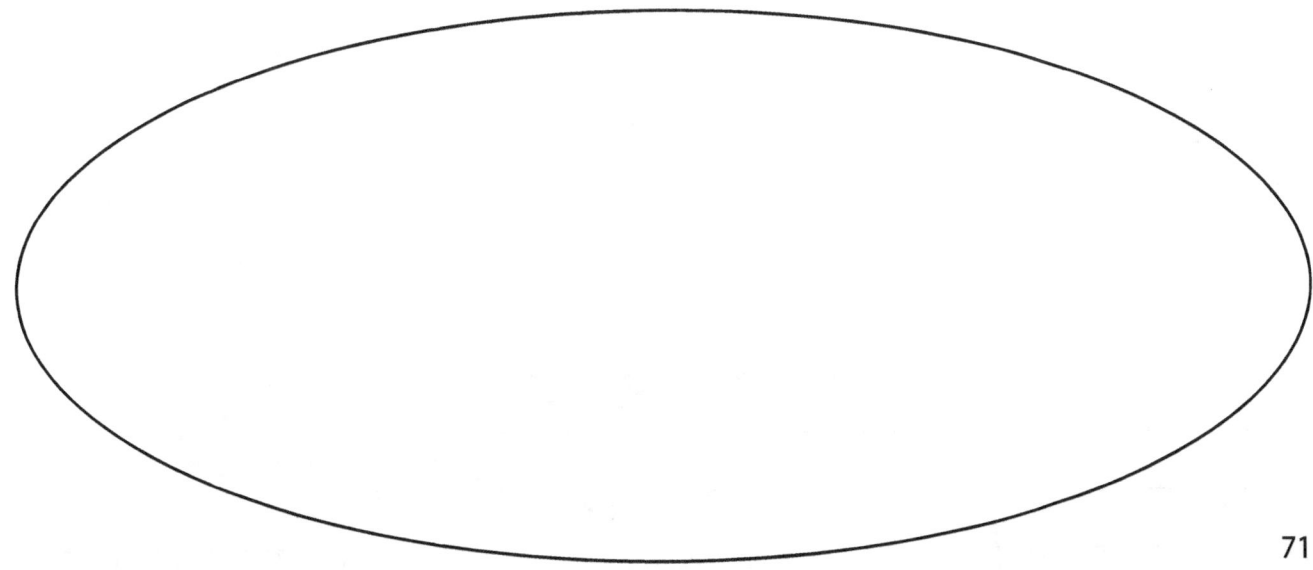

*Happy is the man who has broken the chains which hurt the mind, and has given up worrying once and for all.*
*Ovid*

When I do this it makes me feel happy........

_____
_____
_____
_____
_____
_____
_____
_____

I noticed this went right today.......

_____
_____
_____
_____
_____
_____
_____
_____

## *happiness meter*

date_____

super happy

## I am so thankful for.......

_____
_____
_____
_____
_____
_____
_____
_____
_____
_____
_____

It can only go up from here

## *I saw something that made me smile*

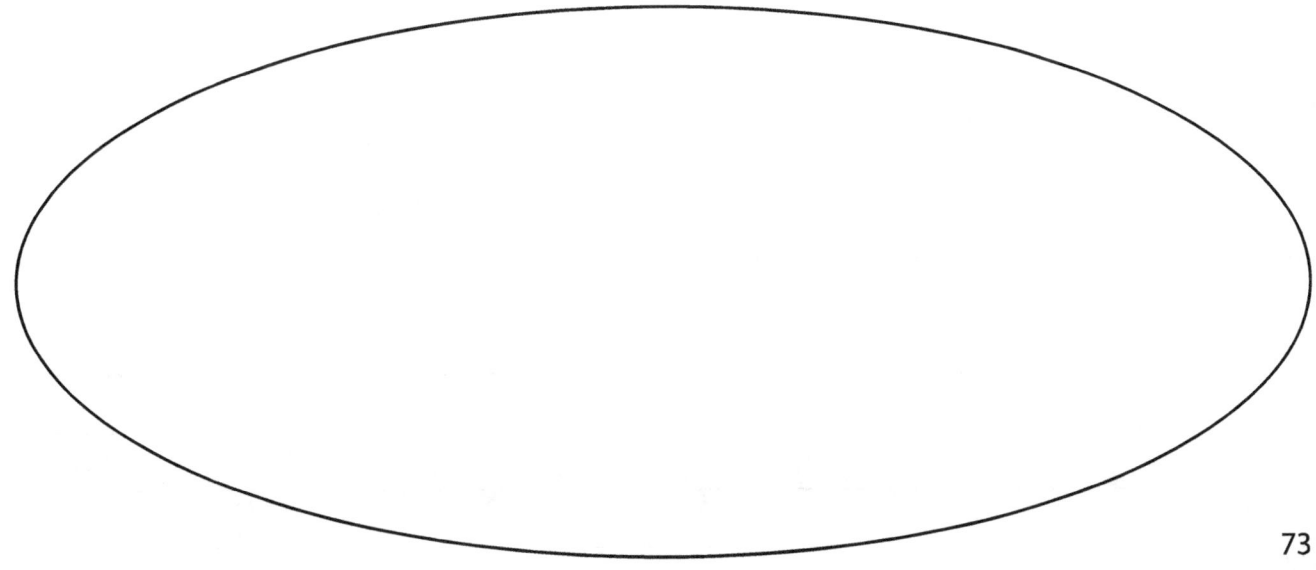

*If you want others to be happy, practice compassion. If you want to be happy, practice compassion.*
Dalai Lama

When I do this it makes me feel happy........

_____
_____
_____
_____
_____
_____
_____
_____
_____

I noticed this went right today.......

_____
_____
_____
_____
_____
_____
_____
_____
_____

# *happiness meter*

date _____

super happy

## I am so thankful for.......

_____
_____
_____
_____
_____
_____
_____
_____
_____
_____
_____
_____

It can only go up from here

## *I saw something that made me smile*

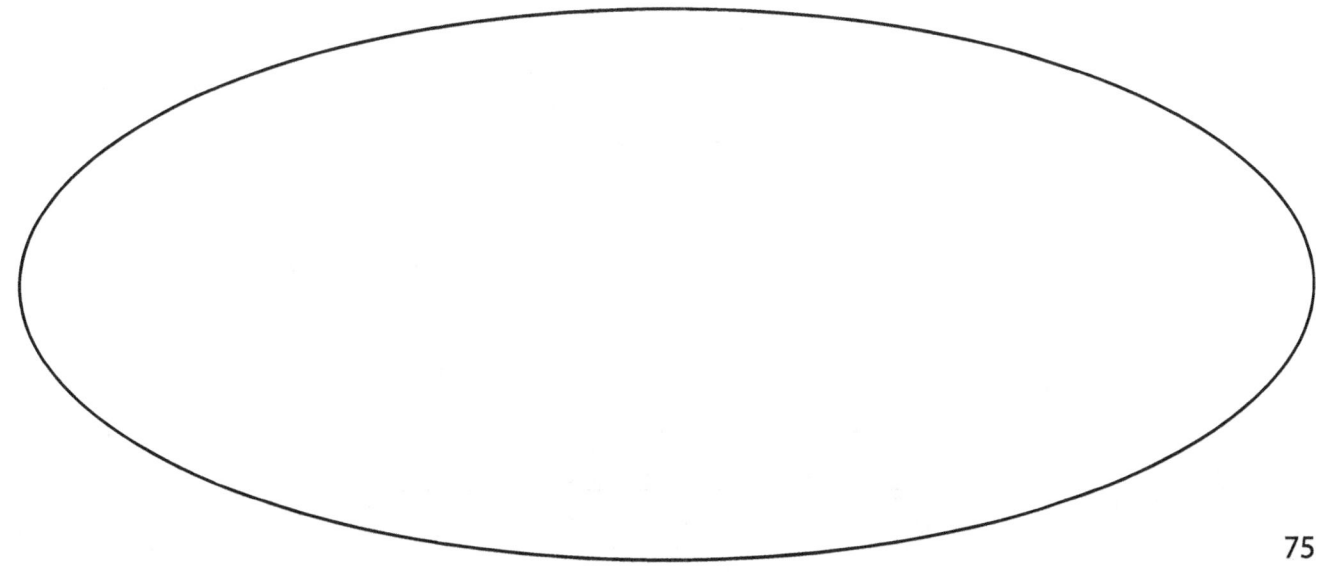

*My ultimate goal is to end up being happy.*
*Most of the time.*
*Taylor Swift*

When I do this it makes me feel happy........

_____
_____
_____
_____
_____
_____
_____
_____
_____

I noticed this went right today.......

_____
_____
_____
_____
_____
_____
_____
_____
_____

## *happiness meter*

date............................

super happy

## I am so thankful for.......

_____
_____
_____
_____
_____
_____
_____
_____
_____
_____
_____

It can only go up from here

## *I saw something that made me smile*

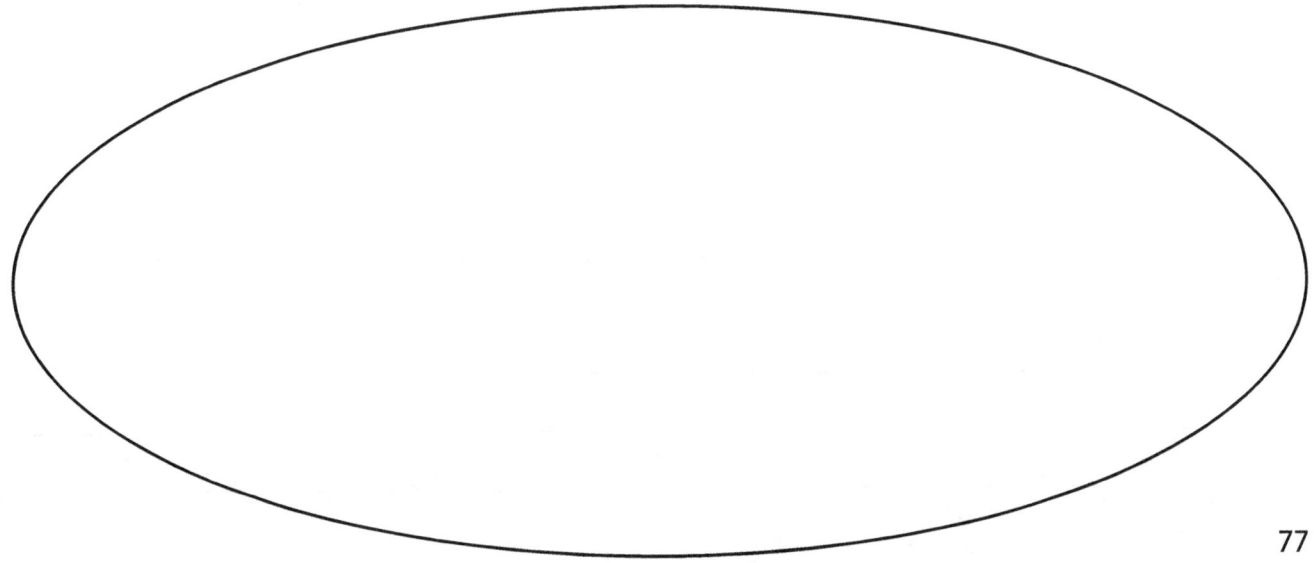

*The miracle is not that we do this work,
but that we are happy to do it.*
*Mother Teresa*

When I do this it makes me feel happy........

_____
_____
_____
_____
_____
_____
_____
_____

I noticed this went right today.......

_____
_____
_____
_____
_____
_____
_____
_____

## happiness meter

date _____

super happy

## I am so thankful for.......

_____
_____
_____
_____
_____
_____
_____
_____
_____
_____
_____

It can only go up from here

## I saw something that made me smile

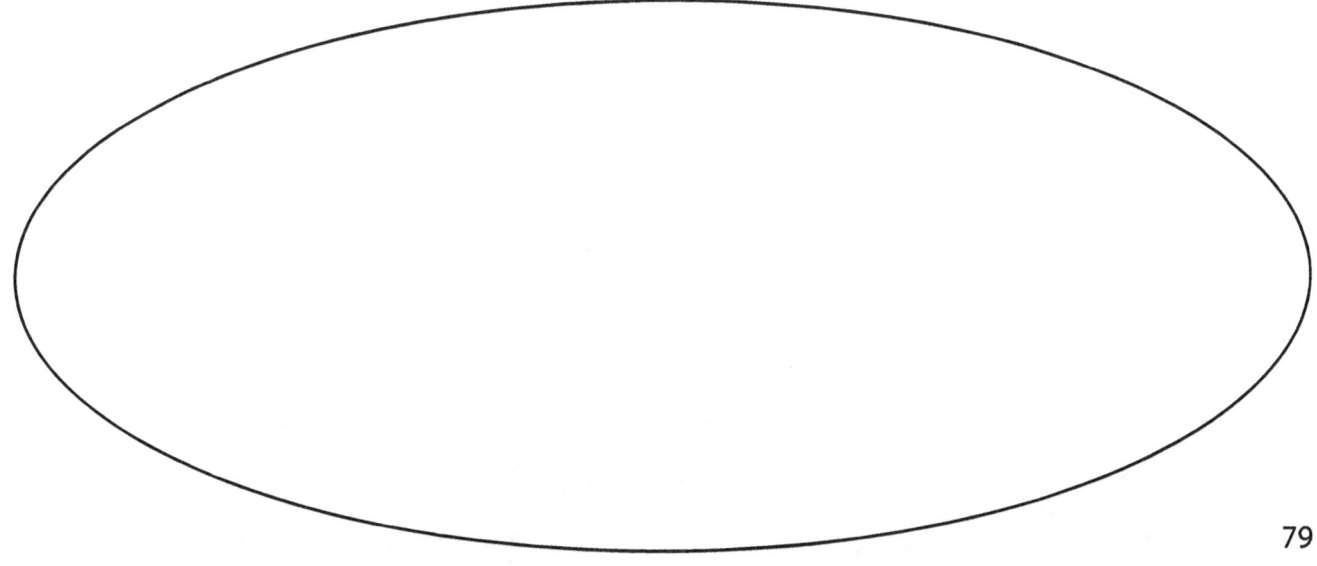

*The talent for being happy is appreciating and liking what you have, instead of what you don't have.*
*Woody Allen*

When I do this it makes me feel happy........

_____
_____
_____
_____
_____
_____
_____
_____

I noticed this went right today.......

_____
_____
_____
_____
_____
_____
_____
_____
_____

## *happiness meter*

date _____

super happy

I am so thankful for.......

_____
_____
_____
_____
_____
_____
_____
_____
_____
_____
_____

It can only go up from here

*I saw something that made me smile*

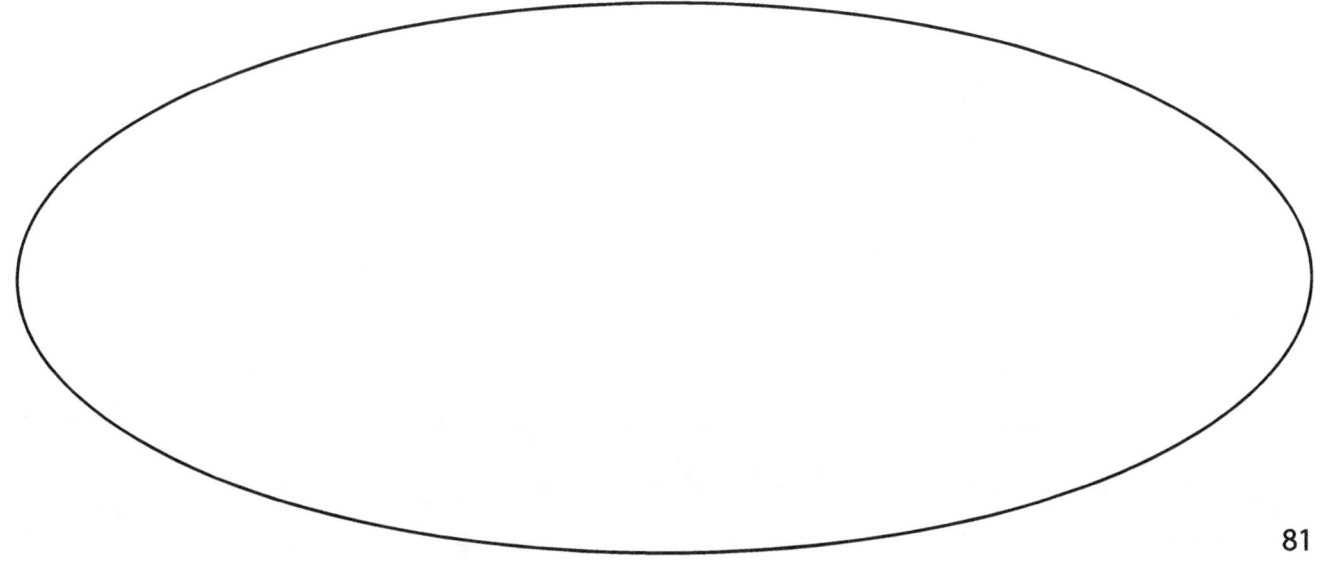

*Watch your manner of speech if you wish to develop a peaceful state of mind. Start each day by affirming peaceful, contented and happy attitudes and your days will tend to be pleasant and successful.*
*Norman Vincent Peale*

When I do this it makes me feel happy........

_____
_____
_____
_____
_____
_____
_____
_____
_____

I noticed this went right today.......

_____
_____
_____
_____
_____
_____
_____
_____
_____

## *happiness meter*

date _____

super happy

## I am so thankful for.......

_____
_____
_____
_____
_____
_____
_____
_____
_____
_____
_____

It can only go up from here

## *I saw something that made me smile*

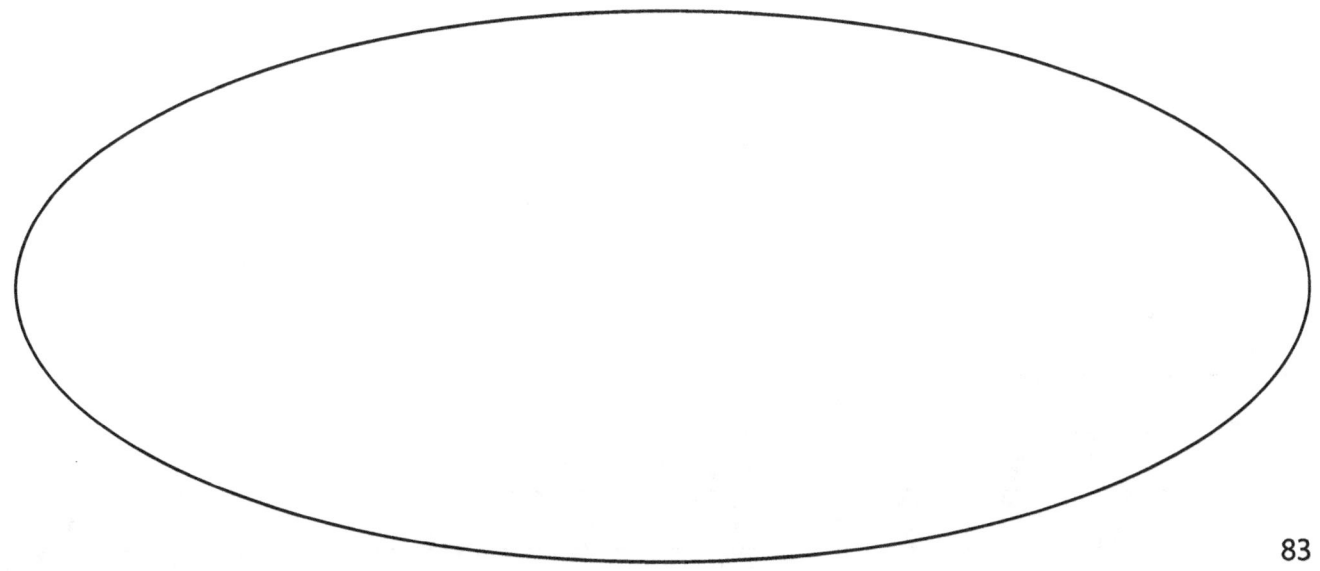

*If you're happy, if you're feeling good,
then nothing else matters.*
*Robin Wright*

When I do this it makes me feel happy........

_____
_____
_____
_____
_____
_____
_____
_____
_____

I noticed this went right today.......

_____
_____
_____
_____
_____
_____
_____
_____

## *happiness meter*

date _____

super happy

## I am so thankful for.......

_____
_____
_____
_____
_____
_____
_____
_____
_____
_____
_____

It can only go up from here

*I saw something that made me smile*

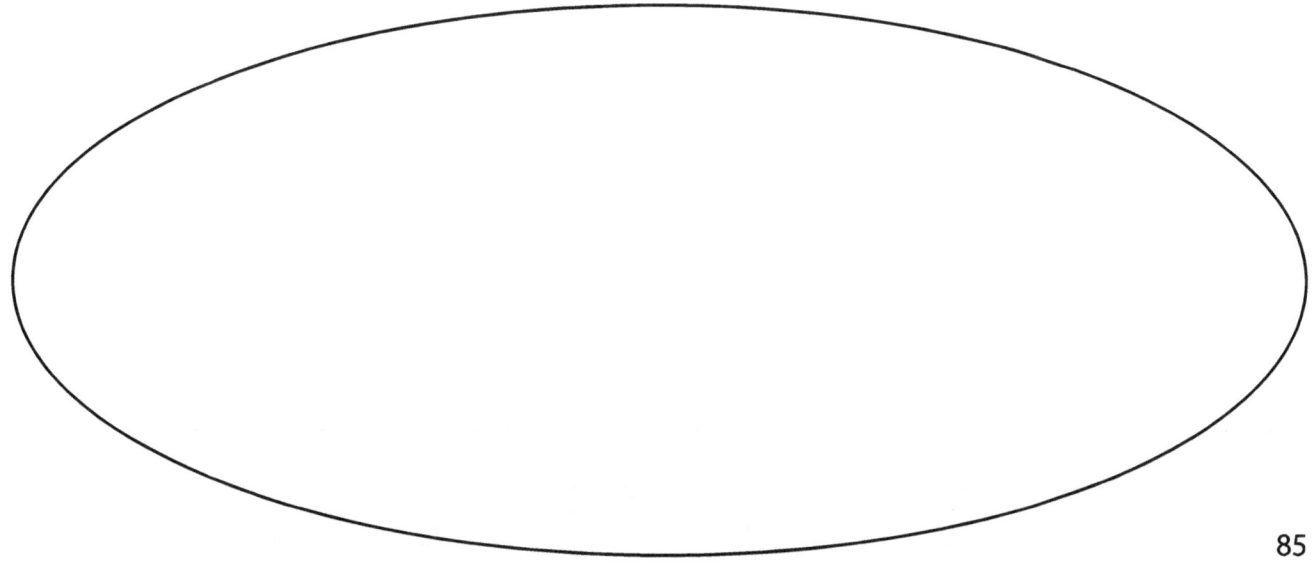

*I have discovered the secret of happiness - it is work, either with the hands or the head. The moment I have something to do, the draughts are open and my chimney draws, and I am happy.*
*John Burroughs*

When I do this it makes me feel happy........

_____
_____
_____
_____
_____
_____
_____
_____

I noticed this went right today.......

_____
_____
_____
_____
_____
_____
_____
_____

# *happiness meter*

super happy

date _____

## I am so thankful for.......

_____
_____
_____
_____
_____
_____
_____
_____
_____
_____
_____
_____

It can only go up from here

## *I saw something that made me smile*

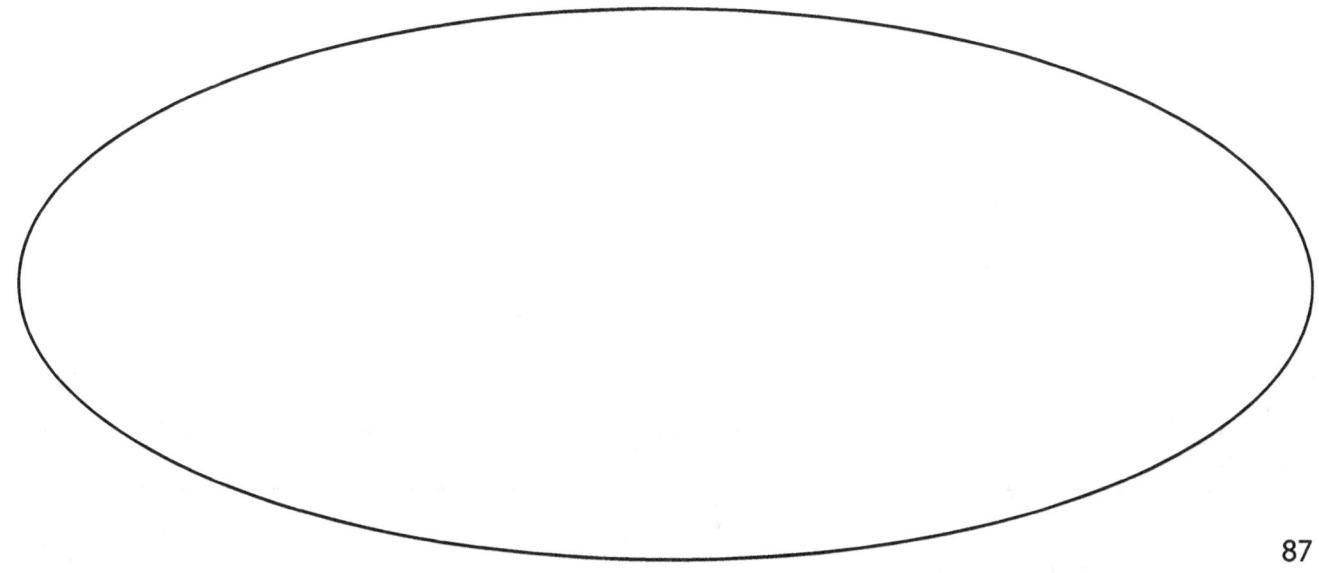

*Life is not always what one wants it to be, but to make the best of it as it is, is the only way of being happy.*
*Lady Randolph Churchill*

When I do this it makes me feel happy……..

_____
_____
_____
_____
_____
_____
_____
_____

I noticed this went right today…….

_____
_____
_____
_____
_____
_____
_____
_____

*happiness meter*

date_____

super happy

## I am so thankful for.......

_____
_____
_____
_____
_____
_____
_____
_____
_____
_____
_____
_____

It can only go up from here

*I saw something that made me smile*

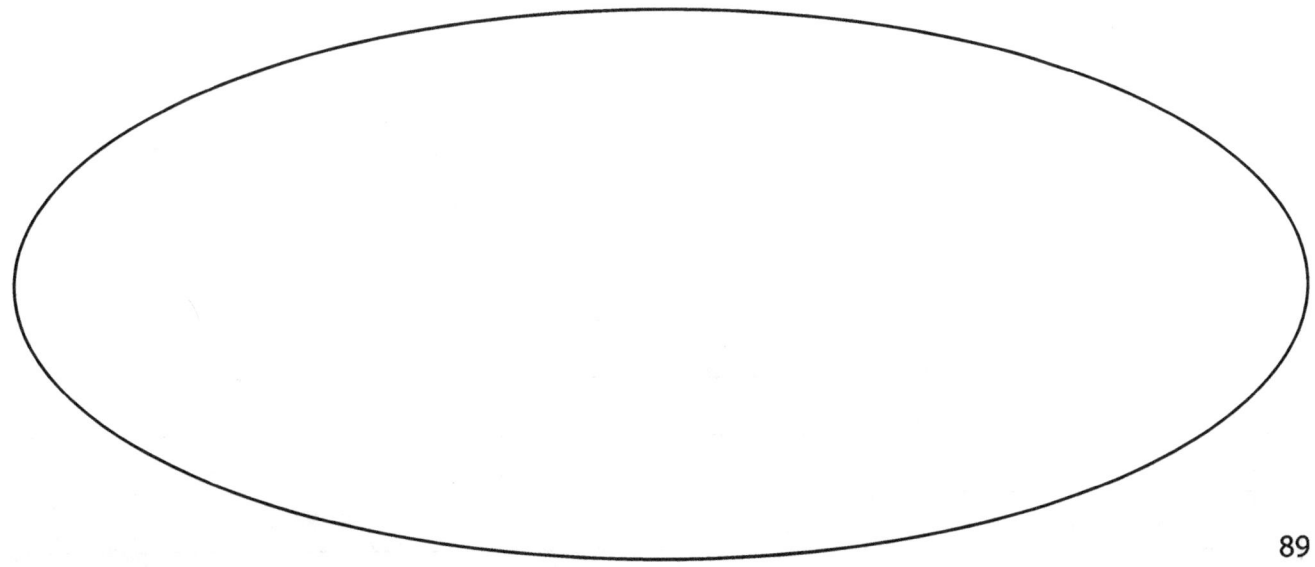

*When unhappy, one doubts everything; when happy, one doubts nothing.*
*Joseph Roux*

When I do this it makes me feel happy........

I noticed this went right today.......

## *happiness meter*

date _____

super happy

I am so thankful for.......

_____
_____
_____
_____
_____
_____
_____
_____
_____
_____
_____
_____

It can only go up from here

*I saw something that made me smile*

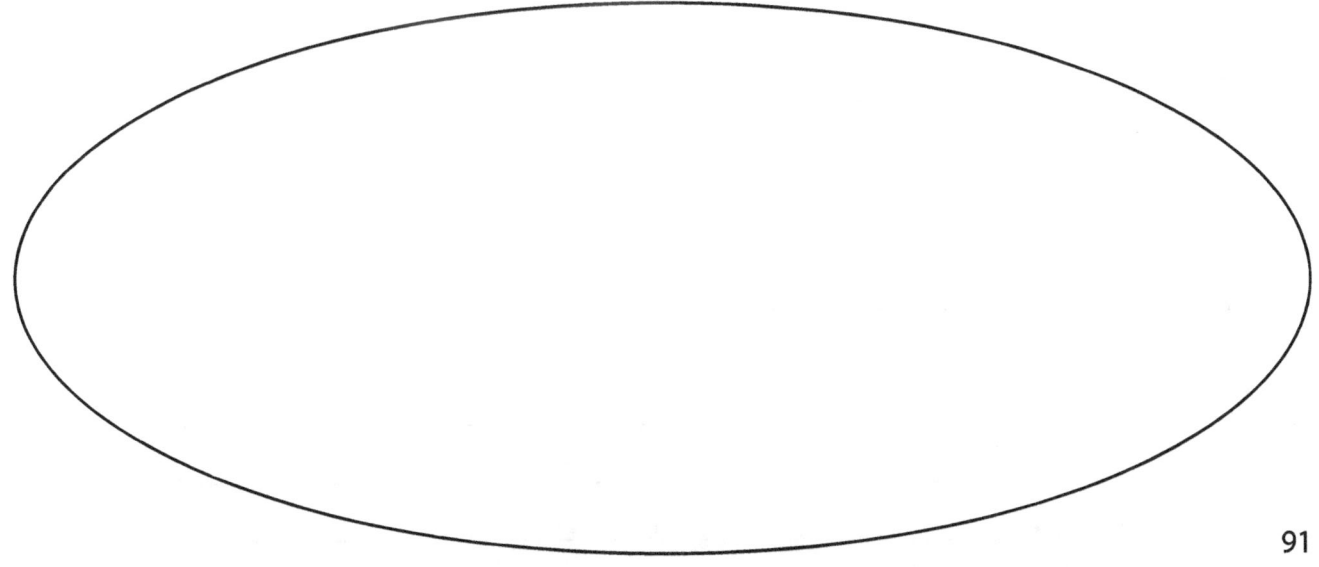

*Simplicity makes me happy.*
*Alicia Keys*

When I do this it makes me feel happy........
_____
_____
_____
_____
_____
_____
_____
_____
_____

I noticed this went right today.......
_____
_____
_____
_____
_____
_____
_____
_____
_____

## *happiness meter*

date_____

super happy

I am so thankful for.......

_____
_____
_____
_____
_____
_____
_____
_____
_____
_____
_____

It can only go up from here

*I saw something that made me smile*

*Cherish all your happy moments;*
*they make a fine cushion for old age.*
*Booth Tarkington*

When I do this it makes me feel happy........

_____
_____
_____
_____
_____
_____
_____
_____
_____

I noticed this went right today.......

_____
_____
_____
_____
_____
_____
_____
_____

## happiness meter

date_____

super happy

I am so thankful for.......

_____
_____
_____
_____
_____
_____
_____
_____
_____
_____
_____
_____

It can only go up from here

### I saw something that made me smile

*It's never too late - never too late to start over,
never too late to be happy.*
*Jane Fonda*

When I do this it makes me feel happy........

I noticed this went right today.......

*happiness meter*

super happy

date_____

I am so thankful for.......

_____
_____
_____
_____
_____
_____
_____
_____
_____
_____

It can only go up from here

*I saw something that made me smile*

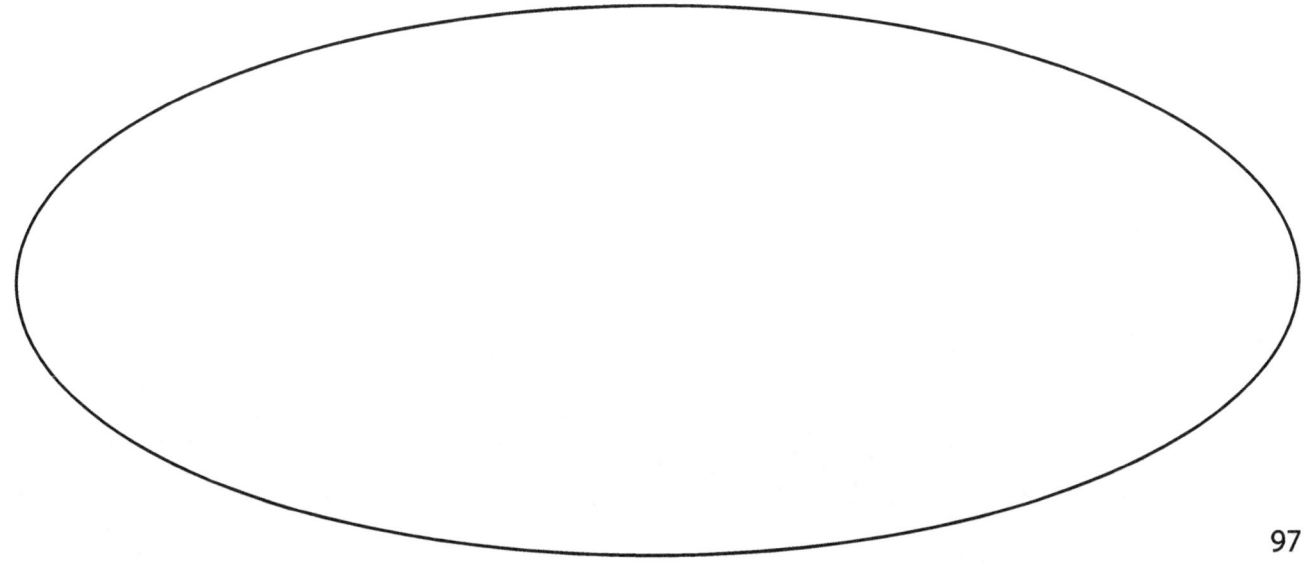

*the extra juicy bits I discovered about happiness*

*the extra juicy bits I discovered about happiness*

*the extra juicy bits I discovered about happiness*

# Available Now
# From Uiri Press

The I Am So Grateful journal is a 35 day voyage into bringing more thankfulness into your life. All it takes is 5 to 10 minutes of daily focus to bring more gratitude into your world.

By Sky Hawk

ISBN 978-0-9979051-1-3

## About the Author

Sky Hawk is an author, artist, nature lover, successful entrepreneur, healer, and mother. She is the creator of her life, the I Am So series, herbal tracking journals, and much more. She helps people feel the love in themselves and is a spreader of joy.

www.ingramcontent.com/pod-product-compliance
Lightning Source LLC
Chambersburg PA
CBHW082227010526
44113CB00038B/2622